HERE, take this gift!
I was reserving it for some hero, speaker, or general,
One who should serve the good old cause, the great
  Idea, the progress and freedom of the race;
But I see that what I was reserving belongs to you
just as much as to any.

Walt Whitman, *Leaves of Grass*

Contents

The Alchemy Spoon
Issue 8: Winter 2022

The Alchemy Spoon
Issue 8: Winter 2022

Editors
Roger Bloor
Vanessa Lampert
Mary Mulholland

A poetry magazine with a special interest in 'new phase' poets

Design and production
Clayhanger Press

Typeset in Times New Roman

Poetry Submissions
Our submission window is next open from 1 – 28 February, 2023

Please read the submissions guidelines on the final page
Submissions are through the website
www.alchemyspoon.org

Cover Images

Front Cover: Chinese Wedding Gift Jar depicting the eight immortals,
Ching dynasty. Wellcome Collection. Attribution 4.0 International (CC BY 4.0)

Back Cover: 'Brown, Black, and White Feather Accessories' by Jennifer
Ben-Ali

ISSN 2635-0513
ISBN 978-1-7391770-1-0

Editorial

In 'The Uses of Sorrow' Mary Oliver writes, 'Someone I loved once gave me a box full of darkness. It took me years to understand that this too, was a gift.'

It is my pleasure to welcome you to issue 8 of *The Alchemy Spoon* with its theme 'Gift'.

Poets sometimes say they don't know where a poem came from, it 'just happened', a bit like receiving a gift. Jane Hirshfield describes poetry as a release of something previously unknown into the visible: 'You write to invite that, to make of yourself a gathering of the unexpected and, with luck, of the unexpectable.'[1] Gifts are freely given, intended to bring joy or pleasure to the receiver. When Anne Carson was asked if she saw the composing of poems as a gift, she replied she did, in so far as it was an attempt to make sense of something to someone else.[2] Certainly over the unsettling past two years with the pandemic dominating our lives, increasing numbers of people have turned to poetry for the gifts it can offer of inspiration, comfort and empathy.

As we hopefully emerge from the horrors of Covid, the world continues to be in darkness from its aftermath, war in Europe, bird-flu, the devastation of climate change and political uncertainty – reminders that life will always encompass change. Publishing this magazine at the present-giving time of Christmas, it seemed apt to offer a theme that might lend some light. Perhaps poems might even be reinstated as gifts in themselves. Certainly, we enjoyed the hundreds of poem-gifts we received.

From the opening poem, 'haruspex' where the poet finds a bone china mug with a lipstick stain, the poems gift us with breathtaking journeys: 'Aladdin inheriting/ unknown skies all the way to a slipper moon', we encounter 'a hula girl in snow', a 'marcasite hat-pin', follow an *acorn* path in the Dales, give ice cubes to orchids, watch a football match, enjoy the gift of sound in a blackbird's song. We 'plunge through the blue-tiled Moorish arch/ into a bee-hum of people', meet a nurse who carries Nembutal on her and discover the joy that can result from eating a boiled egg with a silver spoon. As John Lancaster suggests, in 'A Thank You To Biddulph Library' on page 18 there is a special gift that results 'from learning by heart from the vision of poets moulding language/ to make sense of it all to *construct at last a human justice.*' We hope you enjoy these wonderful poems as much as we do.

The stunning image on the front cover is of an ancient Chinese wedding gift vase, with Jennifer Ben-Ali's inspiring photograph on the back

---

[1] https://www.psychologytoday.com/us/blog/one-true-thing/201401/jane-hirshfield-why-write-poetry
[2] https://unsaidmagazine.wordpress.com/2012/09/11/gifts-and-questions-an-interview-with-anne-carson-by-kevin-mcneilly/

cover. Our featured poet is Canadian-born Barbara Barnes. You can find her poem in the voice of the daughter of the Greenwich astronomer on page 21 and the link to her reading and discussion of the poem on page 58.

My interview with the much acclaimed Liz Berry, in which she offers uplifting and wise advice to our readers, is on page 52, and this issue's A Personal View on page 48 considers the trials of writing by the award-winning poet, Jane Burn.

Reviews of close on twenty excellent new books are offered by Julian Bishop, SK Grout, Diana Cant, Sue Wallace-Shaddad, Martin Rieser, Roger Bloor and Vanessa Lampert, while Reviews in Brief can be found from page 76.

For the next issue we are pleased to welcome Diana Cant as a guest editor. The theme will be 'Graffiti' and the submission window will open on February 1st for one month. Until then *The Alchemy Spoon* sends you our very best wishes for a healthy and festive season and peaceful new year.

Mary Mulholland

haruspex

on a trestle table
in the street outside the home

the suppliants have laid out
her belongings

unfolded and dismantled
entrails for scrying

clip-ons   an empty dosette box
(*Sunday / Monday / Tuesday*)

paperbacks   enamel brooch
a puppet with no face

                    the sign on the altar says
                        Please Take

my hand finds a mug (powdered bone)
printed with pink flowers

brushes the lip-stain on the lip
last sip of breath   an offering

I take it home and wash it warm
dissolving her to nothing

Katie Byford

Hawaiian Necklace

Strung with beads from a tropical tree
with seven twisted teeth dangling,
it lives secreted in a slender drawer
in a jewellery box beneath my bed.

I wore it once on Halloween,
with a grass skirt, over a turtleneck
and thick white tights – a hula girl in snow.

I liked how it draped light on my neck
yet jangled with jungle thoughts,
this gift from my best-friend's vacation.

Each time I give up hoarding, I think
I might throw it away – costume junk –
except for that swerve across the highway
that ghastly day, its unreasonable snow.

Heidi Beck

I give you ink

Amongst the new leaves,
fresh sheets and clean slates wiped by cloths
 still wearing unwrapped creases
I give you a bottle/cartridge of ink.
A blue glass lagoon/black plastic cube to float your thoughts,
Sediment left to dry,
oak in to paper, reader, observer.
Take care in search of stainless scripts
watch out for accidental finger prints.

Choose either re-cycled paper/
ceramic ink wells with steel point nibs
or a brass levered Bakelite pen.
Pump the blue life blood,
fill the rubber sack with careful strokes.

Let it all flow with saturated thoughts.
Wear away the nibs with well-chosen words,
sentences that skip across the page
and don't look back.
Treat the world to your thoughts,
to notes in cards, stonking stories,
new novellas, flashier fiction.
Fill other people's mouths with your scripts.

You can be the wordsmith's match.
Ignite me
Illuminate the world.

Steve Harrison

Token

Because in my mother tongue
verbs end in *-ar, -er, -ir*

for me, some English words
will never be nouns—

words like star, river,
or fir:

roots packed up,
ready to leave

across the sea
and its salt, often

finding solace
in silence,

at night time, here,
for the taking,

a small token
of distance.

Luciana Francis

Hypochondria in a Time of Inevitable Worry

If I could cough colours,
graffiti them into your heart,

I'd tomato-red your words,
sun your black blizzard
with tomorrow's seeds.

I'd purple-sigh your fragrance
into a cape around your shoulders:
bring passion back into your fashion.

I'd green-hum a cooing
for your middle of the night wakings,

huddle-breathe a blue eiderdown
for you to lie on
as the night skies hum with falling stars.

I'd orange-whisper the pauses,
a polite interjection –
the blush of morning after rain.

Hannah Linden

The Museum of Water

Down to Embankment level
across flagged cobbles,
the Thames to the left,
in lit caverns, water is dripping,
I can hear water,
microphones hanging,
catching breaths, sighs of water.

People have given water –
a gold incense container
from Valysana, Ganges water,
water from Alex the axolotl's tank,
pond water, green, unfiltered,
water that was steam
in a science lesson, assembled
coloured molecules of water
(I didn't bring water)
past, present, future water,
water from the Grand Union.
Ice drilled from the Antarctic
a hundred years ago, water
a mother has brought
from her son's shower – he has
schizophrenia – holy water.

Pour water from a silver teapot
into a stainless steel bowl
and voices rise up, water
paired with water, my hands
are wet, dipping into water,
I can't work out how it's done,
clipped silver water, drilled
molecules, water is singing
in green gold, water from
spattering showers, her son's
breaths and sighs, containers
of voices, tipped and spilt.

Pam Thompson

Gift

I woke up this morning with a crow
lodged in the back of my throat.

I hacked and wheezed for an hour
trying to get it loose and out.

It finally flew away when a blood vessel
burst in the corner of my eye.

And now it returns every night to gently place
gifts of silver onto the back of my tongue.

And it sleeps behind my dark breathing
scratching raw the pink flesh where words form.

And every morning I wake early to force it loose
again from my dark dreams and raw breath.

Eric Machan Howd

Gap

I cycled six miles to surprise him
as if I were a prize or a puppy or a doorstep bouquet
or up-leapt in a sudden-bright bannered room
or a red bow for the untying.

His sunken mouth.
That panic-facsimiled delight.
I'd not known his teeth were false,
this fug of neglect.

A friend who resembled a china doll
said the thought of him *on* me made her sick –
my January Santa, tall as a grizzly,
beard and fingers baccy-gold.

So I didn't tell her he once said
in the whiskeyed timbre of his folksong voice
that I made him feel *lascivious*
and I had to look this new word up – savoured
how it sounded like a snake's blue hiss,

didn't say that the afternoon I surprised him
we bathed as if readying for prayer,
unfolded, with what unfurled of us, the laundry on his bed
where, after, I cradled the dormouse of his softness,
slept.

I am nearing the age he was then.
These days I silence the doorbell,
offer my body only to the sea,
wear yesterday's clothes again

understanding better
he was the prize, the puppy, the bouquet –
best-booted and trying
to hide his teeth.

Emma Gray

Please supply one elephant, the voucher said

The bloodied hole in her ear was larger
than a fist—who could have punched that?
and was threaded with faded red bailer twine,
knotted many times making reins
for the mahout to pull her this way, that,
so the hole was stretched over decades.

Heavy-eyelashed, ochre-painted
pachyderm tail-swishing in the heat
and dust of Rajasthan, May 1988.
She paced from foot to foot to foot as if this
might make madness into a breeze.

Scent of hot dung and dust, blown
from the iron-red desert onto a howdah
that was little more than a lumpy mattress
in moth-eaten calico. Dirt, heat bringing
down the sky like a blanket,
crushing everything from the day.

She lumbered up the steep slope
to the ramparts, her ears pulled back
tightly, her shoulders hit again and again
with a short stick, and we sat atop
sweating and rocking her off balance
like latter-day members of the Raj
who have no business clinging on.

The thin paper of our holiday itinerary
was tucked in a salty backpack.
Today, Jaipur, the Amber Fort,
arrive by elephant —
It sounded so romantic.

Kate Noakes

Spar box

I put a waxing moon and a too-bright sun
in a spar box. They nestled against
sunlight shining on stones from a wall.

I tipped in goodnight sea coal and end-of-day sea glass
and sea itself and waves on rocks.

Before I closed the lid I slipped in some thoughts
of Bede and Kielder skies
a Wallsend dawn and a Wearside beer garden at dusk.

In went illumination from Armstrong's plans for lighting
a house by hydro-electricity and Gertrude Bell's travel diaries

I put flakes of paint from this bridge
and that bridge and sand from that beach
and that beach. I shook it until it settled
and then in the gaps I put light and
shadow and dark and
night and day.

Rob Walton

A Thank You To Biddulph Library

Failing exams at eleven consigned you to woodwork
and Sunday school teachers forcing prayed thanks
to im above for his great gifts that only got you fit
to cut coal at Black Bull pit or saggar pots for bottle kilns
till mother took and joined me to my spiritual saviour

on the way to where on the Saturday morning bus
chapel thoushaltnots sniggered and thought me queer
head in a novel alone with a bag of heathen books
them unknowing the thrill of that lending card
as passport to explore another world to satisfy
a thirst for knowledge born of untrue sermons
and to journey reborn in that reading room womb
where the air was warm and sweet with words

And I came out knowing of science and wars
speaking of lunar mountains and craters
rainforests and deserts and African savannahs
of how to bat like Bradman bowl like Tyson
rich in football wisdom from Stanley Matthews
or spouting about Nietzsche and his not joy
but joylessness being the mother of debauchery
or philosophising on the littleness of man
and greatness in Paul Robeson and Rosa Parks
learning from Shakespeare what this drama means
or finding where I stand in the scheme of things
in Orwell's politics of them and us then for Milligan
to blunt it with nonsense and crease me up
and discovering fiction where a hero taught me
to take care criticising those without my advantages
and it all right to write *horseness is the whatness
of allhorse* and of arcs in urinating competitions
and that there no guilt in touching a back to a quiver
tucking in the label of a smokeblue summer dress
and from borrowed records found the hymns of soul
with love songs for my Dansette to pound out
learning by heart ones like Etta James's *At Last...*

and… the spell was cast for with these insights
that search began for me and above all from learning
by heart from the vision of poets moulding language
to make sense of it all to *construct at last a human justice*

And so thanks to the gifts of that place I am democratised

John Lancaster

Visiting Earth

(from the Voices From The Future series)

I like to visit Earth sometimes; I find
The too-brief lives and simple cares a change
From the infinities in which we range,
We who now live unbodied in vast Mind.

I love to watch the children at a zoo,
Careering up and down, shrieking to see
The strange lives in the weird captivity
They also share… and as their parents do.

Visiting in – of course – a human guise,
I can be young or old, female or male;
Sex, power, seduction never seem to stale,
To give gifts seems fair pay for all my lies.

Sailors and tourists visit and then leave;
It's best their hosts have something to believe.

Robin Helweg-Larsen

from the letters of Margaret Maskelyne, daughter of Reverend Nevil Maskelyne, Astronomer Royal

Flamsteed House
Greenwich Observatory

8 September, 1794.

My Dear Papa,

Nightly God flings a black cloth over our hilltop cage. It is meant to keep us calm. The light from a thousand fireflies slips though the weave. I sneak outside to lie on the purple lawn. Silent as the park deer, I wait for the spinning to begin. You said our moon was to be my teacher while you are gone. For ten nights I have watched its plump face being ravaged by the invading dark. Now it doesn't appear at all. I am alone in this wide classroom. I pray that your Wiltshire moon did not suffer the same fate. Mr. Jones gave me six little moons for my orrery. They circle my second-best planet. Tomorrow I turn nine. It is God's favourite number. Just think of his nine choirs of angels!
Your loving daughter in eternity,

Margaret

Barbara Barnes

Leaven

Kneading dough, she hums
to Joni's *Ladies of the Canyon*.
Fashions loaves
to match her swollen belly.
Cossets an aching back.

Marvels at the mystery to come –
a tiny Buddha
who will tutor her
in spells, ocean ceilidh,
elegies of stones. Acorn tales
unfiltered as the vinegar
of apples seethed by bees.

A mystery she will bind
in scents of roses, milk,
a snowlace shawl
crocheted by a failing aunt
in fading black
with no one
left to pamper.

Acolyte in a sisterhood
of mole-eyed girls,
she will tender
muslin, balm.
Little finger
tipped in honey
for a first sweet taste.

She taps crusts
as if entreating entrance
into a temple to be blessed.
Feigns deafness

to siren fears of the unknown,
chuckles at a jumping bean jab beneath her ribs.
Coaxes loaves out of their cradles.
Murmurs 'come to me *mo chroi*'.

Pratibha Castle

mo chroi [kree] my darling

My grandmother, from whom I learned the word marcasite

She's never without it, a maroon beret, moored on iron-grey curls,
anchored by a marcasite hat-pin, a stab at killer elegance,
lest we forget she came from better things.

We sense her disappointment, her vexed confinement
in a small apartment crammed with Art Deco figurines,
tapestries, a silver tea set, trappings of a former life.

Upright, imperious, she doesn't like us much,
never really liked our father, except she'd finally borne a son;
she pierces our teenage giggles with her gimlet stare.

We wear best clothes to visit, quietly waiting for Earl Grey tea,
served in proper cups with saucers, with evaporated milk.
But – and how much this matters –

she makes almond shortbread to die for, always bakes it
when we come; if we're good we get two pieces,
her tasty bait that can sometimes seem like love.

Today, though, she's energised, her eyes are shining –
This nice young man took me out to tea, she announces proudly,
and we had macaroons. He took me down to Weymouth

and we watched the tide come in. We're struggling here,
she's been housebound all year, but now she looks so well.
A polite young man, such charming conversation;

clearly he's found favour, better behaved than us. She beams
with pleasure, her eyes are softer, her beret slightly askew.
He promised to come again next week

but I don't know who he is. Today no almond shortbread,
just the fading fantasy of macaroons. Months later,
in her will, the unexpected gift of a marcasite hat-pin.

Diana Cant

blackbird's poem

only   at the glamorous hour
                    violet   laundered in sheets
            across the lawns
    when pitch   leaks from the woods
                        and moon-metal
                    sharpens the cloud

at the mutable hour
            as windows stream   in the viscous air
        when flowers
                        thin
                    float out
                            on the dark's slipways

what is it
        no thicker than a rabbit's listening
                            presses back
            pushes the heart's sheath: sound
                            o p e n

Lucy Ingrams

Solitaire

Yes, it's my till-receipt
from that coffee we never went for.
An odd thing to keep, but I knew right away.
Remember how I insisted we go Dutch,
how we sat outside in the sun?
And that cute little dog who broke the ice
by coming to say hello.

Oh these, I brought them back
from that walk we didn't take along the beach.
Here's that flat blue stone with the hole
you said you'd make into a pendant.
I picked these up too, these shiny cowries,
and these top-shells, look, pink, purple and silver.
This strange white one's called a wentletrap.

In pride of place,
the ring you might have bought me –
a classic solitaire.

Emmaline O'Dowd

Extra time

Would you like to see the final? asked my Dad
that Saturday morning in eighty-three.
I've been given two tickets. This was a man
who professed to despise United.
This was a match I knew we would win.
And he chose to spend the day with me
leaving David and Mum at home
with the garden probably needing a weed.

This man who rarely went to London
took the time to figure out which Tube stop
was as far as it was wise to drive
(a task that I still set myself today).
He wore my disappointment at being sat
in safety with the Brighton fans
instead of on my feet behind a goal.
He pointed out Sir Matt.

Some days these things surprise me more
than the match ending up two-all.

Carl Tomlinson

The Gift

I am the ultimate philanthropist
I have a gift for you, for everyone.
In my lottery you don't need to buy a ticket,
everyone's a winner. I have free scratch cards
you don't realise you've scratched.

I offer perfect home delivery
No *Sorry I Missed You* card.
No phone call to make a new appointment,
no online form or tracking
no smart red van.

I may meet you before you expected,
touch your hands, see the family pale
watching through the curtains,
wanting me to go next door, down the street,
anywhere but here

sometimes, a customer
tired of his long wait
runs to meet me, embraces me.
It's all one to me

or the overwrought seize
a parcel meant for someone else
won't let go until I take their hand,
lead them quietly home.

Others say they have met me,
bribed me with a golden future,
slipped my hand, stolen away in the night,
seen their life unfold, been offered a different gift,
a choice, but I don't make mistakes.

My patience is legendary,
some receive my gift not knowing
what they are accepting.

I always find my customers,
though sometimes they escape
for a while, no one escapes forever.

Mine is a gift you can't refuse.
We haven't met, yet.
You don't know me. I am a chameleon,
a shape shifter, a changeling.
You only recognise me when at last,
we meet face
to face.

Rennie Halstead

Your Birthday is Next Week

Throughout the year I've thought of gifts:
a membership to a gym with a turquoise pool,
two weeks in Jaipur with a stopover in Dubai,
a candlelit lasagne dinner and Caesar salad,
while we finish with an orange crème brûlée.
Of course, a latte while we stroll along the Bosphorus
where we'll gaze at gulets with their lateen sails,
slipping through waters linking East to West
under a canopy of clouds hinting of unicorns,
ancient philosophers with curling beards.
For you, a thunderhead edged in gold confirms,
bows, beckons with indigo. *Hop on.* And so we do –
without a visa – like Aladdin inheriting
unknown skies all the way to a slipper moon.

Tim Waller

Walking the Dales

after Seán Hewitt

For seven days the carved *acorn* was *way*
for you and me in tee-shirts and shorts,
the September sun on us, our backpacks.

From Grassington to Buckden, Cowgill
and Dent, Sedbergh and Kendal, on foot
we went as three, our *acorn*, you and me.

Done in each day, so exhausted we floated,
could only manage one pint, before falling
asleep fast in our hostel and B&B beds.

Guiding star, carved, we held it close
for acorn was *thought*, was *hope*, small nut
of oak, our *constancy*, *reassurance*.

Cupule and pericarp, testa and plumule,
it was *acorn* that kept us safe from tarmac,
traffic, close to cows, teased us with bull.

A single seed, its leathery shell – we
looked out for it, and it us, for seven days,
acorn our *direction, acorn* our *embryo*.

Paul Stephenson

Chekhov's Stick

Some days we have no visitors, says Svetlana.
My guide longs to escape provincial tedium,
and dreams of English palaces. Like *Irena*,
she sighs, *Ah, London, London, London...*

In the room– a washstand, a samovar, a desk.
Its net curtains catch the Yalta light.
By a coat rack in the corner, Svetlana
recounts domestic tales. Without warning,
she places Chekhov's stick in my hand.
I stroke its elegant malacca, its silver top.

His tragicomic tales of ladies with dogs,
drunken hussars, station masters
and three sisters who long for change.
Petty follies of a bourgeoisie teetering
in the shallows of revolution's vortex.

Ah Svetlana! Your London… my Yalta.
I return my hero's totem, to its place
by his coat in the corner.

Rachael Clyne

Whale-fall

After weeks of mutterings of tides,
chandlers, barrel builders, of him judging
harpoons, of their home strewn
with charts, she's weary, skin and bone.

She turns away from dark waters, has no need
to see his greedy boat surge down the Firth.
Like the whales she knows its sails, their flying
speed that carves wakes, announces death.

Now she'll unlace convention's whalebones, seek
the succour of alone, breathe perfumed loam.
For thinning moons there'll be no presence heavy
beside her. For singing season all will be hers.

Not until blood soils the silver of the Tay and
his vessel returns corpse-laden. Callous handed,
he will be fresh-tattooed. She hopes at least
for gifts of ambergris among the baleen and barrels.

Finola Scott

An Illustrated Guide to the Birds of Great Britain

the gift is not a book
the boys who give it
look hungry for guts
the type who learn
through touch
the gift is not a book
tailed by a warning
do not open at school
the dustjacket finches are liars
covering for a moonflower
that waits for the night
to bloom
the gift is not a book
it's a cuckoo's egg on the shelf
after dark filling his dad's house
with the unfamiliar sound
of women
the gift is not a book
it's boys at the back of a bus
the yield of a lonely village
who never talk about books
but want to know which page
he finished on
the morning flex of word play
blue small starts with t
ends in t bang between no Miss
just talking about birds
Miss
the gift is not a book
it is learning hunger
learning to stare
without threat
at the heavy wattle
of familiar bodies
the gift is not a book
it is something hatching

Spencer Wood

My friend brings me back a scarab from Egypt

It fits in my palm like a computer mouse;
I slide it over the coffee table, listening
for the satisfying *click click* of mandibles,
admiring its gaudy carapace.
The scarab is lapis lazuli blue, looks nothing
like its ancestor chipped from desert glass.
I love its imperfections: little beetle god;
exoskeleton sectioned by uneven grooves
in a botched attempt at symmetry.
All day it naps on a shelf; weary traveller
in a dusty museum of forgotten trinkets;
conkers, porcelain birds, a lump of amethyst.
At night, it scuttles through my dreams;
bright as the full moon over Luxor,
wings deployed like clingfilm sails
to roll its precious cargo across the sky,
then scurries back to stillness like
one of the mice on the mouse organ
when Bagpuss yawns and falls asleep.

Corinna Board

Bequest: a small tin of carved bone fishes

De Reszke / the aristocrat of cigarettes / 50 Virginia

Slender and red-eyed ringed with black; smooth and satisfying
between the fingers. They look sly and happy. Each fish is
hand-painted with a slightly different expression. Over the years
I match them to my lovers, and give one to each on birthdays.
This one's yours – to keep in your pocket or the inside of something.
A reminder of that slat of time when we slipped between the rocks
and flicked our tails.

Rachel Goodman

Her Prayer Book Was Frayed And Held Together With String

I was always first in line for a treat
from Granny's purse. A bag of sweets
or a few coins for my money box.
If I was misbehaving or being bold
she'd wave at me with the sally rod,
but never use it. I was her favourite.
My brother and cousins never stood a chance.
After Grandad passed, I stayed with her at night.
We'd chat and play hands of whist or rummy.
Before bed, she'd insist we kneel for the rosary,
then boil up a sip of milk in the pan to help us sleep,
and a hot water bottle for her feet.
I was twenty-seven when she died.
We hadn't talked properly in years.
Alzheimer's jumbled the words in her mouth and ears.
But as soon as she was gone I believed
she could hear me again. I'd talk to her,
tell her things about my life. My sentences
would trail off into the silence.
One time I faced a problem I couldn't figure by myself
and asked for her help.
I wept as I spoke, told her how much I missed her,
had been missing her for many years.
At that moment, amidst my prayers and tears,
a 'Thank You' card fell from the chest of drawers
and landed upright on the floor by my feet.
Sometime later I relayed this story to a priest.
He wondered if I'd brushed the card with my arm
on the way past, or perhaps a window was open
and maybe there was a draught?
I asked Granny what she'd make of faith like that.

Niall M. Oliver

Ice Cubes for Orchids

Even when I've lost track of days, I know
when it's Wednesday, the day I give ice cubes
to my orchid.

It's not that I'm a fan. I'm not. Yes, some call them
beautiful. Exotic, erotic, delicate, temperamental.
Like myself (I'd like to say), except I'm neither
exotic nor delicate, though I can be

quite temperamental. Just ask my husband, that sweet,
long-suffering man who gave me this small plant that sits
in its translucent container by a window, out of direct light.

It needs diffuse lighting; like me, can't take
full-on sun, never could, always preferred
gray light, the half light, rain and the mist light.

He gave me this orchid plant for Valentine's Day
more than four years ago, when I hadn't the heart
to confess I've never liked them. He's never liked
ice cubes, prefers his water at room temperature.

An orchid needs ice cubes one day per week.
Each Wednesday, I crack out
two cubes from their blue plastic tray, wedge
one on either side of the dark green leaves,

softly encourage the little plant, so stubborn
in its faith, much like my husband, gentle,
quiet and unyielding in his devotion –
to his wife, work, family and friends –

to the plants in our garden, indoors and out,
no matter how ragged or withered, how on the verge
of perishing we might be: as long as one leaf
lingers alive, he will continue to tend, to care,
to love.

Carole Greenfield

The Gift of Deuteranopia

Without you, I wouldn't have learnt how to love
burnt umber, raw sienna, taupe and terracotta,
how to tell fawn from ecru, sand from khaki,
beige from buff or lovat from cowpat.

I wouldn't know now how to earth-up spuds,
or soak brown-speckled beans before planting,
how to use a wooden dibber and coarse string
as a guide for sowing seeds in straight lines.

Without you, Dad, I wouldn't have passed
on your bequest, or accepted my son's belief
that every tree, bush, blade of grass and leaf
was biscuit-hued: morning coffee to bourbon.

If not for you, I wouldn't have discerned,
at a glance, which were his paintings at school:
oatmeal fireworks on black sky, seaside scenes
with green beaches, Cotswold landscapes

transported to the Sahara or Kalahari.
But I'd also have failed to share your
delight at the first celandine of spring,
your thrill at amber and gold in autumn.

Without you, I wouldn't have inherited
these sepia photos in brown leather albums,
nor your favourite mustard-coloured cardigan
with buttons like small, scuffed footballs.

Sharon Larkin

Let it Be

(The Beatles, Lennon–McCartney: 1970)

You gave me this gift,
this elusive wrap of lyric.
I remember sleek vinyl
like otter skin
in the slip from sleeve to deck,
needle poised in semibreve-breath
before the crackle found its groove.

I savour the riff
A minor   D minor   C major
descending to root,
chords familiar
beneath fingers on strings
like a sigh exhaled
at the end of a prayer.

I have met my Mother Mary,
usually in the tip-toe-creep to dawn.
I have heard her whisper,
felt her heartbeat
in the slow of time
like silence after ceasefire,
an offering: Let it Be.

Kate Young

Honeymoon

Much of the Japanese style she finds unsettling.
In Miyanoshita it rains, he explores the curio shops,
she has a cold, stays in their rooms,
the view of Mount Fuji obscured by mist.

The little vase her husband brings her
has a peach-bloom glaze. Sturdy, intimate,
it surprises her. She cups it in her hands,
absorbs its glossy, satisfying roundness.

Peach-bloom, ripe-peach, crushed strawberry
beauty's blush, drunken beauty, baby face
baby mouse skin, copper-freckle, bean-red
powder-red, elm bark, horse's lung
donkey's liver, ox-blood, big red robe...

To recite these together
is a delightful way to fall asleep.

Margot Myers

Babouche Slippers

We plunge through the blue-tiled Moorish arch
into a bee-hum of people – dim corners
stabbed by sunlight, women swathed to their eyes.
Gone, all points of the compass, the city walls,
the certainty of maps.
                              A torrent of bodies sweeps
us past Berber carpets, lampshades
hung from balustrades, hookah pipes, djellabas,
cheap electricals.
                    Abdul's red fez
rolls and dips
through the surge as he scoops pinches of turmeric,
holds up whole nutmegs: *fine, very best –*
his hands caressing the wares as he might a favourite daughter.
                    Children spring out
of doorways, demand *dirham* in shrill voices, push fingers
into our pockets, giggle, what a game!
          Abdul reappears with sprigs of mint
                    against the tannery's reek,
leads us towards
a terrace of vats that gape ox blood red,
burnt gold, chefchaouen blue –
men knee-deep, hauling animal skins by the scruff of their necks.

When we reach the promised marquetry shop,
Rashid pours a miraculous stream
of sweet tea
into small glass cups.
It's time to squat, talk numbers, bargain
with those fine eyes, the subtle geometry of his mouth.

He unclasps an exquisite chessboard, inlaid with silver
and four kinds of aromatic wood.
Chess pieces lie tumbled together in dark seclusion.
He raises the price when I lower it,
then throws in
a pair of babouche slippers:
a gift, because you please me, very much.

I lean in,
inhale a forest of scents.
How easy it would be to accept all he offers.

Claire Booker

So now they're mine

I walk past the window in Rome
each day for a week I walk by
and look at the beautiful shoes
I cannot believe I shall buy

each day for a week I walk by
to admire the flare of the heels
I cannot believe I shall buy
something so lovely for feet

to admire the flare of the heels
I have to loiter and smile
and let myself be seduced
by marbled blue leather and style

I have to loiter and smile
back at the shoes on display
which wink and whisper to me
all you need to do now is pay

Gillie Robic

The Perks of Possible Euthanasia

The woman from Exit arrived
an Italian bag over her shoulder
– a mother of three married to a chef.
She was taken in by the charm my father
reserved for strangers, he spun out her visits
for a year – he was nearly prepared to die,
after his children's holidays. How thoughtful he was,
brave, she wrote to me in an email. He bought her
an occasional flute of champagne by the lake,
slipped her small gifts of money for her time.
She whispered to him of the Nembutal
she'd bring him in a phial.

Hélène Demetriades

Exit – an assisted suicide organisation based in Switzerland

Letter to My Father

That wild day and choppy lake was all ours.
Your smile pinned to this moment.

My birthday treat to spend those awkward hours
with you.

Between Bowness and Waterhead   your salt-
cracked hands rowing   me holding the Kodak Brownie

for the shot of you   your white shirt collar
hugging a paisley cravat   Old Spice

to windward   your woollen jumper –
leather-patched elbows ingrained

with evening tobacco. How rare you were.
I couldn't head off the storms –

my mother's air of anger never far away
sharp as a circling pike.

Forty years later I'm reading your letter
remorse between the lines

too late to tell you   but if
I could have this gift all over again.

Kerry Darbishire

Sky in your mouth

In Madrid at breakfast
in the Hotel Palace
a marvel presents to me:
the entire crystal dome above
is reflected perfectly in the curve
of my silver spoon
upon the white linen tablecloth.
Light blue with spots of green
in the sparkling palm of the curve,
not round as above
but with the shape of a pointed egg.
And as I move the spoon
the blues dance,
the cupola deforms
within a chalice.

I take up the empty spoon
and turn to my small child:
here, taste the sky in your mouth.

John Martin

A Personal View

Jane Burn articulates her views on notions of courage, permission, poetry, and the search for the writing self

Hibernaculum
\hye-ber-NAK-yuh-lum\

Noun

A winter refuge built from leaves and other materials

Somebody once said that we are all meant to have a book inside us.
I don't know if this is true, or what kind of book they were referring to
either— a novel? A pamphlet? Maybe they meant *book* books—

r e a l l y l o n g books, built from bazillions of words
(like *Don Quixote*),   or
memoir or biography, history, science, space, politics.

Maybe something off the beaten track—

      coming out in 2023 from A. Press! *100 Mismatched Socks*
      I Found Under My Bed.

Maybe I should be writing that instead.

I'll tell you a secret. For as long as I can recall, I have wanted to be a writer.

Others have said that we are all meant to have a book inside us but in many
cases, it ought to stay right there. I don't like that—folk might get to thinking
their own inside book isn't good enough. It might stop them writing it. Write
yours, if you can—at least it will ease that itchy pen.

What if every one of us *does* have a book inside, but some don't know how
to let their books out? This is a complex thought, awaiting exploration in a
book of its own.

I'm thinking here of confidence, support, belief, accessibility.
Gender, socioeconomic status, equality, discrimination, resources.
I'm thinking of **Imposter Syndrome** —

a creature that chooses form according to your own worst fears. It tells me that I will never make it as a writer. It can see I am thinking of it, even when I pretend I am not. Despite much success with my poetry, I suffer this creature every day.

> Words, however, appear to be its kryptonite—
> the more of them I read, write, use and understand
> the potential of, the more it is subdued.

I really wanted to let my *book* book loose from where it nestled inside like a hedgehog, hibernating.

Why not [I told myself] stop wondering what sort of book a body is meant to write and put *something, anything* down?

> Write as and when the ideas occur to you—
> whenever you have feelings you wish to express,
> or you find subject matter you are interested in.

I began to uncurl my words onto   Shy Scraps Of Paper
and stuffed them under the bed. I was like the fairytale pea princess, vertiginous atop all those layers.

A major barrier for me has been **permission**. I needed to give myself permission to write. There are many factors out there already, conspiring to prevent you—the past, class, self-esteem, earning a living, caring, responsibilities, health, stress—must you (I told myself) add yet another barrier? **Permission**, for me, has been about pushing on through, being kinder to myself, kicking myself up the bum and taking baby steps into the wonderful, terrifying territory of writing.

Giving myself **permission** was fundamental. It's no good other people telling you YOU CAN DO IT, if you won't tell the same to yourself. There will always be battles to fight in, so don't be your own worst enemy.

Be your own best friend.

49

I came from a home where books and reading were not prioritised, yet I can't recall a time when I didn't adore books. I craved books—the catnip of their smell, narcotic joy of their feel, their weight. The headiness of….well, you get it. Thank heavens for the library, two miles' walk away. For charity shops and jumble sales.

When I was about eleven, my older brother borrowed Tolkein's *Lord of the Rings* from the library. We marvelled at how thick it was. This was my first real contact with a *book* book. I don't know if he ever finished it. When the time came to return it, I promised that I would do it myself.

I thought I'd be able to read it in a couple of days and pop it back, with nobody the wiser. I failed. I couldn't understand so much of it, that it defeated me. I hated it. It made me feel thick. I stuffed it in a corner and went into denial. Weeks later, I was Found Out. There were fines to pay. I got yelled at. This book really *was* about the powers of darkness.

I did not let this book defeat me. I put a few years of graft in before

I COULD read it.

It felt like a massive victory. Every few years, I read it again, to remind myself I am capable of more that I think. Sometimes, these mountains need a bit of time and work before their summits can be attained.

Every time I witness someone describing a childhood of reading, of access to shelves full of well-worshipped tomes, of discussing books at the dinner table, I feel cheated. I feel a sense of loss.

Envy too. We're allowed to have emotions.

I cure myself with thinking how grateful I am that I can do it now. I look at the shelves of books that I own. I have forced the scales to balance a little more my way. I found that poetry is a brilliant means of making me pick up a pen. I dabbled with its wonders when I was a teenager but poetry, I believed (like archaeology, skiing and cravats) was intended for someone else, and not for the Likes Of Me.

I wanted to be a writer. I just didn't know how.

I didn't think it could be as simple as picking up a pen . I wasted years in jobs I hated, made decisions based on stubborn denial of my heart's desires,

50

and vented frustration through self-destructive behaviours. My undiagnosed autism left me vulnerable, unsupported, struggling, lost.

I dipped in and out of other poets' books. I met poets. I talked about poetry A LOT. I began to live. I became obsessed. I fell in love with poetry's searing gems. Finding it was a miracle.

I forgot about *book* books. When the pressure [I had put myself under] to produce that novel or fail was removed, I experienced the freedom of flitting from verse to verse as I pleased. I spent a decade

Getting Serious About Poetry—
wrote hundreds, thousands of poems,
learned how to submit poems to magazines
and anthologies.
I did a pamphlet, then some collections.
I won poetry competitions.
I did guest readings.
I did an MA in Writing Poetry.

Perhaps it's the joy I find in poems that differentiates a poetry collection from a *book* book for me. Perhaps, if I crack the code of *book* books, as I have cracked the code of poetry collections, they will cease to have this curious hold on my mind. They will just be books, and I might write those, too.

I shall add this essay too, to my achievement list. I still wonder when I will, with any degree of confidence, refer to myself as a writer. Is this essay permission?

Am I a writer now?

Jane Burn

The Interview

Liz Berry, winner of the Geoffrey Faber Memorial Award, the Somerset Maugham Award, and the Forward Prize for Best First Collection 2014, and the Forward Prize for Best Single Poem, 2018, talks to **Mary Mulholland**

MM: Do you come from a literary background?

LB: I was lucky enough to grow up in a house where poems, music and stories were valued. My parents both loved poetry. They came from working-class backgrounds but were teenagers in the 1960s when amazing things like The Liverpool Poets were happening and there was lots of crossover between poetry and music.

My mum worked in the libraries in Wolverhampton, so I was always in the library. My dad loves poems too. From when I was young I started learning poems by heart, and he encouraged me to write.

MM: Any particular poets, early on?

LB: We had a beautiful anthology, *The Swinging Rainbow*[1], with everything from Dylan Thomas and T.S. Eliot to folk songs and playground rhymes, so I came to poetry in a very democratic way. Maybe that's why I've always loved poems with a feel of music.

MM: How do your poems come about?

LB: Unless it's for a commission, I almost never sit down and think about writing a poem. It's an exploratory playful process. I've always been a furious keeper of notebooks, and write most days. When I get that 'poemy feeling', when a thought, idea, image or line comes to mind, I will write and write. I find that very freeing.

MM: You capture vulnerability beautifully in your poems. 'The Republic of Motherhood' has an amazing line: 'I prayed in that chapel of motherhood, that whole fucking queendom.' How has motherhood changed your poems?

LB: Motherhood changed me fundamentally, so changed my poems. After my first son was born, I was frightened I'd never write a poem again. I'd had a difficult pregnancy and first year and felt completely raw, rattled by

---

[1] *The Swinging Rainbow*, ed. Howard Sargeant (Collins Educational, 1984)

the anxiety of living this new life. I wasn't sure being a poet and a mother could go together. It took a while to work out how to inhabit that world.

Actually, it was a small but kind permission-giving from a poet-friend, Roz Goddard, that made the difference.

The Black Country came out around when my first son was born. I was feeling lost about my writing, worried people just wanted me to write sweet, joyful poems. Roz said, 'I don't think of you as a sweet poet at all, Liz.' And she was right, that wasn't the essence of my work. That enabled me to lean into the heat and fury and bewilderment, and begin writing again. It made me more open to vulnerability as a poet. I became attuned to my own vulnerability and tenderness, and that deepened the poems I think.

MM: You manage to look back yet avoid nostalgia. I wonder how you do that? Does it connect to what you say about writing poems you'd like to read?

LB: We need and make different poems at different times. When I was writing poems for *Republic of Motherhood*, I wanted poems that acknowledged the rawness and vulnerability of body and soul, to be true to that. That's why I had to write them in that time, that urgency. I had a toddler and was pregnant again, so it was written in a heightened state.

I'd wonder why there weren't more poems about birth and the early days of motherhood. Later I came to realise that by the time most women feel themselves again and able to write, the heat has passed. My sons are five and eight now and I feel so differently. You have to catch the moment, even in a notebook, as it might be gone in the future.

MM: You mention soul, and I notice a thread running through your poems, for example, 'Our Lady of the Birth Trauma', 'Our Lady of Psychosis', and your references to birds, often seen as a symbol of spirituality. Can you say something about this?

LB: I am deeply interested in matters of the inner being, or soul. I'm not particularly religious, but poems occupy that space for me and allow me to reach towards a feeling of something that's within, beyond, that we don't fully understand, something holy. I am especially interested in exploring the souls and inner worlds of women; almost creating an alternative universe, a spiritual universe, that holds women very carefully.

And the birds, well I'm enchanted by them. Birds represent otherworldliness, and escape, they're part of both sky and earth, spirit and body, flight…

MM: Do you regard yourself as a feminist writer?

53

LB: I definitely describe myself as a feminist and therefore also a feminist poet. My feminist beliefs and values inform everything I do, and I'm especially interested in the lives and history of women: their journeys, bodies, their longings, how patterns are made between generations...

We often perceive the Black Country through images of traditional masculinity (such as heavy industry, working men) so I'm curious about how the feminine exists within and in opposition to that. I look for the feminine energies in the region and how these might be disruptive or transgressive. I speak about *feminine energy* as I'm also interested in the crossing of boundaries and things that nudge at perceived borders (male/female, animal/human, domestic/wild).

MM: You write about desire, the body and sex in a very visceral way. How easy is it for you to be so open?

LB: In my notebooks I'm my truest self. Because they're so private, I can be uninhibited and uncensored. I wouldn't like anyone to read them, but they are the documents through which I might best be known. For me, there's often a long journey between notebook and poem. I spend a lot of time working on my poems and drafting them, sometimes months or years. In this drafting I'm able to decide what I feel comfortable with showing. I'm very private, especially over the privacy of my sons. Reviews of *The Republic* highlighted that there's little mention of a partner or baby. That was a deliberate choice, a way of drawing a circle of privacy around my family.

I feel fine writing about sex or sensuality, perhaps because the self in the poems feels different to the me on the school run or pushing swings; poems feel like the place where I can allow myself to explore the wildness.

MM: I read you were afraid of how 'The Republic of Motherhood' would be received.

LB: That was probably the hardest poem I've ever published. When *Granta* accepted it I rang my friend, Lucy Mercer, a fellow poet and mother, in tears, worrying that people would think I was a terrible mum or that my sons would grow up and read the poem and think I didn't love them. There's so much shame and anxiety around new motherhood, of being lost or not coping.

But when the poem was published, it felt electric, for months (even now) I was flooded with messages. It seemed to allow people to speak about something which had felt unspeakable and to feel less lonely.

Yet as I was putting together the pamphlet I was still hampered by anxiety, trying to soften it or add poems which felt sweeter or more acceptable. But my brilliant Chatto editor, Parisa Ebrahimi, helped to keep me true to my vision.

MM: That leads me to ask how you know who the right person is to turn to for advice.

LB: Never be afraid to ask for advice. Try and work out what you need help with (form, drafting, courage) and seek out help from someone who is brilliant at that.

For the book I've just finished, a narrative sequence due out in March, I had help from several poets: Hannah Lowe, Fiona Benson, Jonathan Davidson, Declan Ryan. Each reader brings a different skill and a different set of advice which is invaluable.

MM: I also wanted to ask about your use of dialect: how do you decide when, and how frequently to use it?

LB: I just listen to the poem and see what it wants.

MM: Another thing is your use of names. One of my favourite poems is 'Christmas Eve' where we encounter Mick and Eloise, and Eloise turns up in another poem.

LB: I can't tell you all my secrets, Mary! But it gives me a special pleasure to sneak in people I know and love, though I almost always change their names.

MM: I've not mentioned your humour, the light touch of 'Our lady of the hairdressers'...

LB: I never think of myself as witty, so maybe it's more a general warmth towards my reader. I'm mindful of this in my readings too. When I first started doing poetry readings, I was so nervous that I machine-gunned the audience with poems! Then I heard Simon Armitage say that the chat around the poems is a way of being kind to the audience, building good feeling. It's all about how you shuffle the pack too – sometimes you might choose a funny, joyful set, and other times a set that is moving or unsettling.

MM: What about turning points in your poetry career? How important has recognition and winning prizes been?

LB: Whenever I've won an award, there's a moment of genuine surprise and disbelief. When you're nominated, you're up against brilliant poets, any of whom could win. It's like a lucky dip. I can say this because I've been on all sides, winning, losing, judging.

I always keep in my head: *make hay while the sun shines.* Enjoy the recognition (and the work it brings) when it's there, as there may be quieter years ahead. Love the poems and keep that as your priority.

Honestly though, the recognition that means most comes from readers. It's my favourite thing when readers write to me about poems which have touched them.

MM: Regarding disappointment, I've heard you say, 'be fearless and kind', but how, in practical terms?

LB: Write the poems you have to write. Don't feel you should write poems that are fashionable. Write for pleasure, be fearless, but also kind to yourself. Keep the poets and poems you love in your heart and take courage and comfort from them. On days when it feels hard or you feel discouraged — and we all have those — step out of poetry into the world beyond. Go for a walk, cuddle someone you love, listen to a song – to put it into perspective. Years ago, I taught some teenage girls and we talked about this. One of them gave this advice: 'It's just a poem, Liz, not your whole life!'

MM: Who are your favourite poets?

LB: I love and need different poets at different times, discovering new poets, keeping old favourites close. I seek out poets who have the energy I need: is it a joyful energy, or sensual, or someone to meet you in your sorrow?

MM: You mentioned earlier your new book, *The Home Child*, how did that come about?

LB: *The Home Child* is a novel in verse (a book of poems which tells a story). It's inspired by the life of my great-aunt Eliza who was a 'Home Child', one of thousands of vulnerable British children who were emigrated to Canada to work as indentured farm labourers and domestic servants. The book follows Eliza from the slums of the Black Country to rural Cape Breton; a journey I followed several years ago when researching the poems.

I was so moved by Eliza's story, and those of Home Children like her: the way their lives were flung about, sending them so far from home, and how they managed to survive. I began writing a few poems, and that grew until the sequence was book-length.

MM: Did she write letters, or is this from your imagination?

LB: The story is inspired by true events and the first-hand accounts of Home Children but it's a work of imagination. In many ways, Eliza's story is deeply sorrowful, but I wanted to use the poems to bring something different, a sense of her wonder and inner being, all the fizz of being twelve.

MM: Is there anything you might add specifically to our readers, many of whom came to poetry following other careers.

LB: I love working with poets who've had another life before poetry! I know people often feel self-conscious about coming to poems late in life but think of all that richness you bring. Zadie Smith calls it 'the education of the heart' and I love that. You're never too late for the poetry party!

MM: Can you sum up what poetry has given you?

LB: So many things! As a writer: a sense of freedom, an ability to express myself and explore. As a reader: comfort, inspiration, understanding. Good poems constantly reveal new things. Poetry has also given me meaningful and precious friendships.

MM: Do you have a favourite poem of your own?

LB: I feel very tenderly toward 'Birmingham Roller' as it's given me many gifts and reached so many readers. It was the first poem I wrote in dialect – making the language of my home the language of poetry. 'Birmingham Roller' has found itself in all sorts of curious places: on a bench, an album, at christenings and funerals, a jeweller even made a brooch inspired by it. Imagine: a little concrete pigeon's egg!

Mary Mulholland

Publications by Liz Berry
The Patron Saint of Schoolgirls, 2010, Tall Lighthouse, £8.19
The Black Country, 2014, Chatto & Windus, £10
The Republic of Motherhood, 2018, Chatto & Windus, £4.25
The Dereliction, in collaboration with Tom Hicks, Hercules Editions, £10
The Home Child, forthcoming 2023, Chatto & Windus, £12.99

The Reading

Watch the video

Barbara Barnes reads and discusses her poem
'from the letters of Margaret Maskelyne, daughter of Reverend
Nevil Maskelyne, Astronomer Royal' which you will find on page 21 and
'I am Twenty', a poem from her collection *Hound Mouth* published by
Live Canon 2022.

The Alchemy Spoon
YouTube Channel
https://youtu.be/8_QuU9K9aKE

Reviews

Julian Bishop looks at a distinctly contemporary take on spiritual verse which spans 43 centuries of writing and a debut pamphlet from a well-established poet

Kaveh Akbar
The Penguin Book Of Spiritual Verse
Penguin, £20 (hardback)

Claire Collison
Placebo
Blueprint Poetry Press, £6 plus £2 p&p

While the title may not excite, the editor most certainly does – Kaveh Akbar, the Iranian-American poet and academic whose *Calling A Wolf A Wolf* debut was quickly followed by two Pushcart Prizes. Predictably there's John Donne, William Blake and George Herbert but thankfully he's cast his net much wider than that. Anyone for Wislawa Szymborska, Li Po or Sappho?

He's honest in the introduction: 'I've no idea what I mean by God and I say it a lot.' He has a stab at it though, suggesting these poems seek to thin a partition between the self and a divine, whether that means God, family, sex or justice, 'a shared privileging of the spirit and its attendant curiosities.'

The book is beautifully presented. Each of the 110 poets and poems featured gets a brief introduction on one side of the page, the poem on the other so you don't have to keep flicking to some appendix at the back, one of my pet hates. The poems span some 43 centuries of spiritual writing starting with a Sumerian priestess called Enheduanna, priestess to the goddess Inanna, translated by Jane Hirshfield which ends 'My beautiful mouth knows only confusion/ Even my sex is dust.'

This entwinement of the erotic and the divine underlies some of the other standout poems. I'd never heard of the South African poet Ingrid Jonker whose poem 'There Is Just One Forever' begins: 'Ochre night and your hands/ A vineyard through summer and frost'. It's a gorgeous poem and perhaps the greatest value of this book is the insight into Akbar's own tastes in poetry. I'd highly recommend it for anyone wanting to stretch their poetic horizons a little more, even if a chunky volume of spiritual verse sounds daunting.

Some poems surprise on the page too. Fragments of Sappho translated by Anne Carson snake down the page with blanks where the text is missing, allowing the reader to fill in the gaps:

```
]
] work
] face
]
]
if not, winter
] no pain
```

Similarly striking on the page is a tenth-century piece by Al-Husayn ibn Ahmad ibn Khalawayh, who plays with the 99 names of God in Islam in a poem (?) called 'Names of the Lion'. Among some of the highlights for me were:

al-Miktal	'The Big Food-Basket'
Dhü Libd	'Whose Hair is Matted'
al-Jayfar	'Whose Sides Are Well Filled Out'
al-Ashra'	'Whose Nose Is Long and Prominent'

One surprising but welcome entry is a late John Clare poem, his deeply painful 'I Am!' with its acknowledgment of the 'vast shipwreck of my life's esteems' which nevertheless attempts to end on a relatively optimistic note: 'I long for scenes where man hath never trod/ a place where woman never smiled or wept/ there to abide with my Creator, God.'

Others take on a contemporary resonance which harks back to one of Akbar's points that there's a universality to much good poetry, be it spiritual or otherwise. Osip Mandelstam died in a Stalinist labour camp and his brief prayer merits a full page in the book. It's translated by W.S. Merwin and Clarence Brown:

O Lord, help me to live through the night –
I'm in terror for life, your slave:
To live in Petersburg is to sleep in a grave.

If there's a criticism, it's the inclusion of works that read more as contrived instruction rather than poetry, e.g. a poem by Sengcan, a sixth century descendent of Buddha, whose 'one is all, all is one' mantra comes across as clichéd. And Psalm 18 ('The Lord is my shepherd') might deserve its place but obviously displaces work that might come across as fresher. Akbar acknowledges this conflict, blaming either a finite permissions budget or simply the fact that 'I claim no objectivity'.

And I suspect some poems are included more because they're simply very good rather than ticking the divinity box. One poem comes to mind called 'Rainbow' by the Haitian poet Paul Laraque which is full of great imagery:

> It is a ribbon tied to the rain's hair
> It's a multicoloured belt round the waist of a little darling
> It's a talisman to chase the evil eye away
> It's a lasso round the sun's neck
> to make him come back and light up the earth.

Apart from a derivative ending that echoes Rilke's 'you must change your life' it's an example of a poem you probably wouldn't come across anywhere else. The sheer range and scope of this book is enough to make it worth a read.

ﮢ

The first poem in this pamphlet – Collison's debut – is appropriately about a lemon: sharp, with a zing and tingle that makes you smart. The same could be said about most of the poems here where no word is wasted and many contain a sting that lingers long after. To quote the above poem 'see how lemony it looks/ inside!'. There's also a very attractive colour graphic of a lemon inside the cover.

A lot of the poems describe the ordeal of having breast cancer but even here, Collison's wit and sharp observation lift the poetry into fresh, unexpected territory. After a mastectomy there's an appointment with a clearly hot young oncologist whose arm is 'spooning me to him' as she lies down on a couch, with the poem ending 'he captures my heart/ it gushes like an old twin tub', which brought a whoosh of tears to the eyes.

I found myself rooting for her through the various traumas she describes in a disarmingly matter-of-fact way before introducing what I'm going to call the Collison Zinger. An example: the day before the mastectomy she goes swimming in the Hampstead Ladies Pond ('there's a dog show, with celebrities', she recalls) where she meets a woman who's been through the same experience many years ago:

> The scars were old, and she was old –
> and she was here, and swimming,
> pond from the neck down.

That comma after 'and she was here'… plus all those 'and's triggered another whoosh…

Several of the poems revolve around a single image – an eel, an ankle, a pendant, even mozzarella which is reminiscent of the smell of a

61

dead sister. The images are worked hard to take centre-stage in the poem rather than being passing similes, in this case the poem ending with thoughts about the 'signature scent' of the dead: 'white and creamy, floating in brine'.

The acknowledgments at the end read like a *Who's Who* of the UK contemporary scene and I lost count of the number of various prizes and awards mentioned, but she wears excellence lightly. I don't often read pamphlets more than a couple of times but this one's for keeps.

Julian Bishop

Diana Cant looks at a debut pamphlet which uses the setting of a sheep farm to explore the nature of relationships within the larger dimensions of the world

Mary Mulholland
What the sheep taught me
Live Canon, £7

Mary Mulholland's engaging debut pamphlet exists, as all good poetry should, in a number of different spaces. Firstly, there is the taxing task of shepherdessing, with all its vicissitudes and physical demands; secondly, there is an undercurrent of a stuttering relationship, calling the reliability of romantic, sexual connections into question; and thirdly, there is a reflective and distanced rumination on maternal love and the poet's place in their life and the world. Quite a distance of travel in only twenty-seven poems!

The first poem is visually arresting – a concrete poem, wittily delineating the isolation and repetitive nature of shepherding, but also the attendant danger and the need to stay alert. There is a colloquial energy to some of the writing: 'It's no Bo Peep work [...]/ Docile, my foot, they buck and jump like rodeo sheep' and a capacity for observation that captures the 'sheepness' of sheep, as they 'Wander off as if all that fuss was for show.'

This is no sanitised, sentimentalised version of looking after livestock, but a world where hens devour each other's eggs while a crow

> gores a hole in the fleece
> of the newborn for the lungs ...

> & the mother calling   calling
> & her lamb gasping   gasping

The savagery of the natural world is echoed by the accompanying doomed relationship, where blood and sexual imagery merge – 'there's blood on your lips,' ... 'I do not / want to squeeze anything from you.' And later, 'O the toads I have kissed'. Rejecting the romantic, the poet contemplates the power and devotion of the maternal bond, and feels the pull of the elemental:

> this lightness
> attracts me
> the way it shifts
> refuses to be held

as she seeks to find her place in the world:

i am part of the farm.

the sheep and trees are in me, the wind is rising,
blowing straight through me. i can hear the sea.

A word on form – these are poems written in a variety of forms – couplets, tercets, prose poems and sonnets. Indeed, over half the poems here are sonnets, although handled so deftly as not to be immediately apparent. The language is, for the most part, straightforward, although the ideas can be quite complex. Mulholland is a poet who can use form unobtrusively but engagingly, and who can ask some large questions with a lightness of touch.

Oh, and the (sadly unattributed) cover design is an additional delight.

Diana Cant

Vanessa Lampert looks at a collection which explores the nature and meaning of time

Rebecca Cullen
A Reader's Guide To Time
Live Canon, £10.00

'Consider time. The way it collects and stays' asks Rebecca Cullen in this, her first collection, joint winner of the Live Canon 2021 International Poetry Competition.

The book is divided into eight sections. Collectively these poems read as a long meditation with a prevailing theme of the nature of time. Apparently part-memoir, individually the poems frequently free the passing of time from its linear trajectory as they alternate and ricochet between units of minutes to hours, days to millennia. 'Douglas' opens with the speaker's father in later life: 'Suddenly, he's eighty', the poem then arcing backwards in time to close with him now a child:

> [...] Finally,
> he's eight, already wearing glasses. I watch
> my dad like a mother, the spindly legs
> I recognise, his face as he sits, crouched
> beside the wireless, waiting for Zorro.

Cullen demonstrates considerable lyrical skill in economically and precisely evoking the visual. The first stanza of 'The Crossby's, she knew, were deeply resented' reads

> Angela fell for Ralph as he stroked
> his moustache, sluicing
> a single malt around a tumbler.

As evidenced here, well-chosen line breaks illustrate the poet's wry humour. This lightness of touch is also utilised to counterbalance weightier themes of social commentary and feminism. The poem 'Women in Love' begins, 'Endlessly in parlours, waiting in heavy silence/ for the inevitable opinion, sentences repeated'. Written in couplets, the poet builds the poem's theme of rousing defiance slab by slab, finishing by imploring its (female) reader to

> [...] pluck gentians from the rockery,
> red carnations from your décolletage

and batter them. Save up their petals,
make confetti you don't need and point

your life, your flame, in the direction
of your head, and over and over

pour out your gratitude for your escape,
his fecklessness.

This collection's overarching thematic consistency keeps in the reader's mind, time passing, even when it is not directly addressed. In 'Diving Swallow', the athleticism of the trapeze artist is captured as she prepares herself 'with powdered soles, her feet/ palming the rope ladder, each seventh rung/ a pause'. The entire poem holds steady its attention upon the moment before she leaps from the platform, and in so doing seems to hint at how brief her life as an athlete will be.

Also noteworthy is the poet's skill in harnessing the personal and the political, often within a single poem. 'Special' rails against poverty 'where the children's/ lunches come from foodbanks' while also expressing (an apparently personal) wistful yearning for youth: 'We wanted to be older than we were/ to stay like that forever, to snog the fifth years/ riding into school on scooters like in *Quadrophenia,*'.

Rebecca Cullen has accomplished remarkable cohesiveness in maintaining her focus upon perceptions of time in this, her first full collection. Highly recommended beautiful writing.

Vanessa Lampert

Martin Rieser looks at a collection exploring relatedness and identity

Tania Hershman
Still Life with Octopus
Nine Arches, £9.99

Hershman takes us directly into a world where the octopus is both a real animal and a stand-in for her protean emotional self. There are seven 'Still life With Octopus' poems interspersing the volume, which switch between scientific explanation and exploring the internalised metaphor. 'There's an octopus in my chest, trying/ to give my heart to you. She will not listen.' ('Still Life with Octopus (1)'.) The poetry appears to use the literalness of the Martian school of poetry combined with magic realism, to gain immediacy and to also merge the boundary between literal and metaphoric: 'Salt the woman, pepper her children, curl/ the unbecoming husband, refill the dog.' ('And in the Arrangement of Salt'.)

The playfulness of the poet's language is refreshing and immediate: 'So I sit in the waves/ and I wave at the shells// and I shell up my heart/ and I hearten my feet.' ('Fed'.) The unusual inversions of language allow us space for a kind of reckless embrace of these personifications, which in turn opens out multiple meanings for the reader. The body becomes an embodiment of the speaker's contradictory selves: 'You might/ be okay, says her heart. There's room/ for improvement, say her lungs. The liver// claps and nods.' ('Application'.)

The nature of reality is forever being re-examined and re-experienced as in this verse in 'I am Interested':

> I examine my hands as if
> they belonged to someone else.
> I watch the fingers move, ripples of
> skin, the wrinkles that appear…

By the end of the collection a traditional superior view of nature has been reversed; the octopus has become the compassionate sentient being: 'what if instead, they took us/ in their arms, said, We've been watching too' ('Still Life With Octopus (VII)').

The speaker appears to recognise the contradictions in her own emotional self and in humanity's false hierarchies of intelligence projected onto nature, and re-orders them to make the reader question any or all smug certainties and unthinking assumptions. This is a protean work about the ultimate protean creature, ourselves.

Martin Rieser

Roger Bloor looks at a collection exploring experiences around integrating into a new society and culture and returning to one previously familiar

Alexandra Corrin-Tachibana
Sing me down from the dark
Salt Publishing, £10.99

In Corrin-Tachibana's first collection the poet explores experiences of cultural and social dislocation, through the voice of a woman looking back at her marriage and life in Japan for ten years, where everything is at first strange and unfamiliar, and contrasting that with the course of her life following the breakdown of her marriage and her return to England.

The effect of immersion in a different culture for a prolonged period is highlighted in the first poem of the collection, 'Coming Home', when 'home' appears strange:

> I miss *miso* soup for a hangover
> and I miss the word for hangover:
> *futsukayoi* (second day drunkenness)

and again when coming home for a New Year party:

> … stepping out at Heathrow I see Brits
> through non-British eyes. How overweight they are.
> How greasy their Fish n Chips…

Although the collection is divided into six sections, the poems move in an interlocked way to draw out a picture of the light and dark of relationships, slipping smoothly from:

> *Happy Happy Happy*!
>
> Like the little messages
> Pink and white
>
> On fizzy *Love Hearts* sweets
> Children love to share and read.

to the painfully simple and understated line 'Tomorrow we'll go to City Hall on your bike,/ to divorce.', which seems to underpin the sense of the title of the collection, the need for someone to sing the speaker 'down from the dark'.

68

There is a transition across the collection, from a mix of English and inserted Japanese words and scripts, to the final section where the language fades into a more natural and colloquial style, as new relationships are portrayed with a much lighter and relaxed form. The lovers have '....naked tea,/ propped up by Holiday Inn pillows.' or watch 'Miss Haversham on your crappy TV/ your feet up, in kingfisher socks.'

It would be a mistake to read these poems as simply some form of confessional autobiography, this is so much more – there is a depth and honesty in the descriptions of behaviours and emotions which speaks far beyond the personal, immersing the reader in the complex and intimate confusions that are at the core of relationships. This is a collection which uses a well-crafted variety of forms, from Ghazal to prose poem, exposing the raw edges of social and cultural expectations of women within marriage and wider social settings.

The final two poems in the collection move the reader closer to hearing the voice that knows there is a way down from the dark, a voice that embraces the words of TV's Miranda who says '…women should make gallop-/ ing a thing, should gallop' and speaks of the freedom of uncaged nightingales, of how:

> …once these nightingales, caged
> for their song, would kill themselves dashing against
> their rails, trying to fulfil their migratory urge.

From the first poem of the collection 'Coming Home' to the plea of the title of the closing poem, 'Sing Me Down from the Dark', there seems to be one underlying and poignant ambition – to find a resting place: 'where when I say the words/ *I'm home*, I alter your state of mind,' a place where love can finally be 'Unrestrained, uncontainable.', and the *gaijin* (outsider) can be herself.

This is a debut collection that is written with a fresh and confident style. It avoids sentimentality and uses the restless and sometimes unfamiliar patterns within the poems to reflect the uncertainties and paradoxes that inhabit the interior world of endings and new beginnings.

Roger Bloor

SK Grout reviews two collections that consider how a formal aspect of poetry can enrich and give deeper meaning to poetry of the human condition

Mina Gorji
Scale
Carcanet Press, £11.99

André Naffis-Sahely
High Desert
Bloodaxe Books, £10.99

Scale is an ambidextrous word, containing many meanings. This collection is generous and open-armed as it invites the reader to contemplate this multiplicity. There are seven pages of definitions in the Cambridge University Press online dictionary[1]. It's a word that moves between tools of measurement, geology, music, distance, astrology, the body and the human condition. Perhaps it's encountered most recently in conversations about climate disaster – the scale of the problem so immense it's difficult to know where to begin.

Mina Gorji's second collection, *Scale*, is a navigation through these concepts, and more; each poem considers the scale of something, its heft, time and weight, how a body feels when scale is encountered. The poem 'Dream' encapsulates this:

> I am kneeling
> in the desert
> on the sand.
> I can't remember
> any sound —
> just sand.

The collection was written before and during lockdown, and as readers we encounter the concepts of the possibility of scale in its bounteousness, but also the claustrophobia a body might feel in a confined space. From 'The Snail':

> I try to hold
> your presence,
> and feel instead
> the distances
> of stars.

---

[1] https://dictionary.cambridge.org/dictionary/english/scale

These are poems that are slim, and slim-lined on the page, negotiating the rooms of black and white space, both formally in the way poems are constructed, and a number of times in the poems themselves, and how language encounters the page: 'The map reveals' in 'Scale' or 'The Alps/rise up in black and white' in 'The Alps'.

It is a deft and delicate thing, but Gorji manages to create small and intimate poems on the page that, through their preciseness and minuteness, still provide openings for a reader to range out in their imaginings. The language is close, tender, familiar and simple. And yet within that framework, Gorji allows a depth to enter. In the poem, 'MRI' the line 'I can't scan' suggests the machine scanning a body, but also how we might scan or inspect a line, or scan something to prove it. A few lines down 'I can't scan' becomes 'I can't imagine'. There is also an engagement with the scale of time – poems about the Ice Age, seventh century BCE Babylon, 'Plum season ending' ('Half Moon in September'), the time it takes for a spider to weave its web – and space. From 'Yellow Stone':

> sky full of stars —
> the same stars —
> almost the same.

There is too the body's engagement with scale. What happens to a body when it first encounters snow, in 'A Red Door Opens', or undergoes a body scan, in 'MRI'. These poems encourage us to think about the contours of distance, how they feel to us, how do we arrange them in our minds.

At the launch of *Scale*[2], Bhanu Kapil, in conversation with Mina Gorji, remarked on the juxtaposition of the delicate nature of the poems, and how we might imagine this as emergent but also endangered. That something so precious holds precariousness as well. There are poems about tube-worms and wood frogs who have adapted genetically to live in extreme environments; poems about discoveries in melting glaciers of fossils and Ice Age mammals; but also poems about hedgerows, field mice, snails and (from 'At the Edge of England') a formation of flying geese

> is spelling out
> a secret song
> like sacred script.

Gorji invites us, as ever, to engage with the musicality of language, form and subject matter. A scale is, after all, also a measurement of music.

---

[2] https://www.youtube.com/watch?v=8dYijzC6e0w

She practises this not only in the rhythm of the poems, but in the sounds using assonance and onomatopoeia. The poem 'Sediment' contains sibilance, 'Stalks, spines / bone fronds', in nearly every one of its fourteen lines.

Whether subtle or strident, each of the poems in this collection engages with these multitudinous concepts of scale. The poet asks us what is our place in this scale, where is our perspective? Can we encounter and understand different points of view? There are very few poems in the first-person point of view, as if Gorji's view looks outward and ranges across distance. But there is always a centrifugal point too. We are held with generosity within the intimacy of these small poems which are treasures.

შშ

Recently I read James Longenbach's *How Poems Get Made* and, in his chapter on Voice, he argues that poems are driven not just by a speaking subject, but by 'strategic deployments of various kinds of syntax and diction'[3]; in critical discussions on poems, he wants readers to consider that a poem is delivered by a speaker who is not necessarily always a person, but rather a poetic metaphor.

André Naffis-Sahely's second collection, *High Desert*, employs a number of speakers, both reliable and not, to convey messages about the power and privilege of history and the discourse and fragility of politics. The collection contains four sections and a coda with a strong though varied narrative impulse throughout. These are poems where time is a movement – whether the poems are considering the past, the present or the future. They are framed in a way that encounters the moment before collapse, the beginning of the end, bringing into focus the current highly charged discussions about climate disaster or the rise of nationalism against the cyclical nature of history (and nature within a desert). From 'Ode to the Errant King':

> What is a great
> global city, a great country (whatever
>
> that is) without an island
> of tears, a terminal of surrender?

High Desert's first section tells stories from diverse places and times. It rings with polyphonic voices, ranges across the globe from 'The Train to St Petersburg' to 'Chittagong' and roams around the twentieth

---

[3] James Longenbach, *How Poems Get Made*, W.W. Norton, 2018.

century and further back into the establishment of countries and dynasties: 'While the Lombard kings called us seabirds' ('Nova Atlantis'). The second section, 'the City of Angels', feels closer to (a sense of) home, after the wide-ranging 'Peregrinations', because it contains carefully constructed elements of the autobiographical (whether or not they are, of course, is for the poet to know). In the first poem, 'Welcome to America', the speaker faces a number of increasingly disturbing questions from a border control agent:

> What kind of man calls himself
> cosmopolitan? You're rootless
> and dangerous.

The third section, the eponymous 'High Desert', also takes place in the present-day, although the poems broaden their scope to look back at such events as the Spanish Flu, the Great Depression and workers' rights movements in pre-WW1 America. These poems act as reportage to the 'weird, rusty ghost towns' and campaign slogans of 'the Orange Duck candidate' ('Roadrunners'), poems that are witness to a world on the brink of collapse, the end-of-times. From 'High Desert':

> There is no better backdrop
> for the mirage
> of permanent boom times than the desert,
>
> a landscape, where despite claims to the contrary,
> no town was too tough to die.

The final section before the Coda, 'A People's History of the West', contains thirteen found poems created from letters by various American figures of all political and cultural spectra. The first poem is from Pablo Tac, a mid-nineteenth century linguistic scholar of the Luiseño people of California, and the final two poems consider the McCarthy trials and American Communism from two wildly different perspectives: Muriel Rukeyser and Richard M. Nixon. These are extraordinary examples of poems engaging with archive and documentary; the sheer amount of research and dedication further deepens the feeling of witness both to this section, and to the collection as an entity.

Indeed, while I was reading *High Desert*, I found myself recollecting poems and ideas from *The Heart of a Stranger*[4] edited by

---

[4] André Naffis-Sahely (ed.), *The Heart of a Stranger An Anthology of Exile Literature*, Pushkin Press, 2019.

Naffis-Sahely. (The first poem, 'The Last Communist' particularly resonates with a poem by an anonymous miner from Bisbee, Arizona, in 1917.) This speaks to a deep and long-term engagement with these topics as a poet, and a thinker.

The final poem in the collection is a love poem, that still manages to engage with Naffis-Sahely's key themes of politics and their incursions into daily life (in this case, the pandemic), wanderlust for both place and language, and the desert. 'Nothing breaks your heart/ like a small western town'.

High Desert is a collection of docu-poetry, witness and warning. Through narrative and its tools, the collection makes the case for the speaker as device, not forgetting that behind one speaker there can be multiple humans with lived histories. That these are living, breathing entities with desires and frustrations, political motivations, impactful and impacting relationships with nature, as exemplified in 'Chittagong', 'he pretends not to hear me, then, hours later, his reply: ''how do you translate the meaning of horror?''.'

SK Grout

Sue Wallace-Shaddad enjoys the imagery of a well-crafted pamphlet

Jo Bratten
Climacteric
Fly on the Wall Press, £6.99

'Climacteric' means 'a critical period or event' and is also a term for the menopause. The pamphlet ranges across many topics: the body, our impact on the natural world, loss, sins, solace, having a shower and the meaning of rubbish. These often darkly inventive poems demonstrate a rich use of language and skilful poetic techniques.

The opening poem 'New Year's Day' starts fairly innocuously but ends on the words 'a warning'. 'On Flood Street' takes this up in an epigraph, quoting the alchemist Sir George Ripley (1415–90): '*beware of the Floode*'. Written in couplets, the poem is appropriately medieval in tone with words such as 'throttled', 'flayed', 'venom,' 'entombed' and 'putrescent'. The narrator tells the reader: 'gilded prayers leap from lepers' sores/ while asses in high places snuff up air'.

'In the shower with Gerard Manley Hopkins' has lyrical lines full of alliteration: '*Water of world of self-dew, flesh-dew whirled*' and '*Wet wind-washed lovescape manshape rinse and wring*'. The poem is multi-layered, touching on relationships, nature (by implication) and morality: 'I have sinned again'. In other poems, 'Dear Heavenly Father' and 'Searching for God in the Asda Carpark', the poet speaks of prayer and a search for redemption.

Bratten uses rhyme and half rhyme to good effect in 'This is not a ~~love poem~~ poem about the moon'. The first two lines set the scene: 'There's a witch living inside my mouth, bitch/ to the last, she makes freakish demands, shrieks'. This witch seems to represent the challenge of writing: 'she wrestles my pen, spits ink in my face'. An extended metaphor is also used in 'Crab in my hand': 'catch eternity with your claws'.

'Because we have forgotten how to sleep' has fourteen examples of the present participle in this twenty-one-line poem, including one which crosses a stanza break: 'her tentacles slip-/   pering through the yellow spaces of his flesh'. This gives the poem a restless energy. 'Fall' is full of the sounds and texture of 'thomping', 'damping', 'oozing', 'clomping' as well as the 'rasp of rapacious wasp'.

Bratten's evocative images, whether dark or light in character, keep the reader engaged. I enjoyed the idea of 'doomscrolling' in 'Chiaroscuro', 'shadow ends like foundlings' in 'Distancing' and 'drupes spooning in the sun' in 'Solace'. There is much to savour in this well-crafted pamphlet.

Sue Wallace-Shaddad

Reviews in Brief

Ellora Sutton
antonyms for burial
Fourteen Publishing, £8

Though the title suggests an undercurrent of grief, these are also poems of colour, life and love, finding beauty in what has passed. From 'Mood Ring':

> *Orange.*   My mother died a long time ago.   I'm still getting to
> know her ...
>
> ... Some mornings the light through my bedroom
> curtains has my mother's way of singing - softly to the
> escaped peach faced lovebirds nesting in the chimney.

Sutton's exciting images and original use of language make for an inspiring read as she flits, not unlike a bird, from thought to thought. In 'Collective Noun for Birds' the poet writes: 'I think I am really an aviary masquerading as a girl.' She visits an ornithologist, much as one might see a psychotherapist: 'I ask her what will become of the loose net of my body/ when half or more of the birds want to migrate./[...] She says, *a beautiful sky I'd imagine.*'

Images of the sky, together with bold jumps between poetic thoughts, help create a sense of expansiveness in the poems and invite the reader to pause on particular lines, such as, also from 'Mood Ring': '*Pink* The sky is all scar tissue this evening'.

'Underglaze Blue' seems an apposite title for a poem in a book exploring unearthing a burial. 'There are ghost tours/ such magnificent ghost tours,/ sometimes they last for days'. However grief is balanced by its opposite emotion, in the poet's exploration of love, particularly queer love. In 'The First Time She Touched My Hair' there is a skilful lightness in how she describes the anticipation of happiness: 'waiting for my ride, all split-/party bag with queerness'.

Sutton excels in creating intriguing titles, such as, 'Self-Portrait as Obscure Facts, a photo series', in the form of short prose sections with enticing lines like 'Australia is so vast the moon could wear it like some kind of ancient cuff bracelet', and in the final section: 'Titanic survivors remarked upon the brightness of the stars.'

This poet displays a marked athleticism in her use of form. 'Tourist Information' is a sequence of list poems, with some arresting lines. In

'*Water Safety (ii)*': '- Tonight the moon is a goose-head carried about like an empty/ or emptying coin purse'.

There is also the sheer enjoyment of eating sweets, 'so sticky so/ galloping'. Sutton describes 'Starmix' as 'melted hearts/ of glucose syrup/ & fruit juices'. This is a highly accomplished second pamphlet from an exciting young poet.

∽

Kathryn Bevis
Flamingo
Seren Books, £6

Perhaps the most surprising aspect of this pamphlet, considering the list of successes in the acknowledgements page, is that it is Bevis's debut. Her poems are intelligent and surreal, playful and brave. A joy to read, too, for her skill in using language, for the music, and the content conveying the warmth and resilience of human nature. One example is 'Knitting Nan-Nan' where the poet writes: 'My needles click like tiny typewriters and she spools/ from them – her Fair Isle of stretchmarks, her bingo wings'.

This is a poet who seems to enjoy pushing limits in her poetry, and there is real wit in 'The title of this poem is "What's the Title of this Poem?"' in which the poet comments on a poem (written in italics) within the poem, for example: 'Next, a stanza of rich description, all *glittering tarmac/ and streetlamps haloing the night.*' Bevis boldly presents 'Matryoshka' as a centered poem; this is a wonderfully effective poem about childlessness with decreasing stanza lengths, and the smallest 'wood all the way/ through'.

One contender for my personal favourite is 'My body tells me she's filing for divorce' an extraordinarily powerful poem in which the speaker considers her treatment for cancer as if she and her body were separate entities: 'The worst thing is she doesn't tell me straight up to my face. No,/ she books us appointments with specialists.' The poem ends with the narrator's body in bed, while she herself is 'flying, crying/ looking down, *Too soon,* I whisper to her warm/ and sleeping form, *Not yet. Too soon. Too soon.*' Similarly, in 'My Cancer as a Ring-Tailed Lemur: 'We both know one day she'll eat me.' The poignancy such lines achieve is heart-rending and moved me to tears.

Another of my favourites is 'The Smuggler': 'She knew she'd need to start off small so took the spoons/ What a boon!' The subject, supposedly trying to extricate herself from a seemingly abusive relationship, takes more and more of their joint belongings, 'Today's his birthday and she's carried off the roof,/ the rafters, chimney pot. So what?' And the triumph of the ending 'Of all the things she ever took it was her ma's/ advice that got her out', leaving him 'on all fours, howling at the moon.'

There are also poems steeped in love and tenderness, such as 'Honeymooners' Ghazal', 'You teach me the name of each bird, my love/ and I test on my tongue every word, my love'. These are defiant poems, unflinching, they exude warmth, beauty and pathos in equal measure.

∞

Eds Ruth Sutoyé and Jacob Sam-La Rose
Before Them, We
flipped eye publishing, £11.99

This wonderful anthology of 24 British-based poets of African descent explores the lives of grandparents and elders.

The opening poem, by Tolu Agbelusi, 'Tell Me All the Stories, This Time I'll Remember', engaged me at once: 'When I meet my grandfather for the first time,/ he has been dead for almost a hundred years.' The speaker learns his grandfather sewed 'another patch //onto the threadbare agbada, the only one he owns' and told his son (Agbelusi's father), *'Poverty is a thing of the mind'*.

Each poet's brief introduction about the inspiration behind their poems is equally absorbing. On the subject of his great-grandfather, Gabriel Akamo writes, 'All I know about his life is how he lost it'. Esther Kondo says: 'I remember visiting a grandmother once. I say a grandmother because she was not my grandmother, but she was a grandmother, and I called her grandmother.'

Dzifa Benson explores the loss of her Ghanian language, Ewe, in her poem 'Echolalia: a Broken Rule Ghazal'. It opens 'This is the place. I am here. These are their names, unsaid in water'. Several poems similarly use images of water. In 'learning to swim', Asmaa Jama writes: 'my uncle was a boat freshly carved, beautiful in water.'

There are prose poems (such as 'autopsy' by Asmaa Jama) and praise poems (such as Thembe Mvula's 'Praise Poem for Makhulu'). Be Manzini writes about the magic of the liminal space between truth and dreaming and how 'I jigsawed pieces of stories'. In 'Gogo':

> My father always spoke of you
> in English; my heart listens
> in Ndebele. I call you Grace
> in both languages.

Not only are the poems in this anthology beautifully lyrical, with striking content, sound and images, but several use highly original form, such as Ola Elhassan's 'Atbara as Coefficients' in the shape of a coefficient matrix holding the scattered information about her grandmother, alongside places where she had lived: 'Edinburgh, London, Khartoum, Atbara.'

Michelle Tiwo employs the use of erasure for 'This, Is All I Have', explaining that working with space emphasises and highlights 'what happens to rich (hi)stories, when little was shared and the imagination has to fill in the blanks'.

The inclusion of eleven pages of striking colour photographs of African women is explained in Sutoyé's foreward as being images from a multidisciplinary project of which this book forms part.

The poems are also infused with wisdom. Damilola Ogunrinde writes how spirituality and silence are embedded in all aspects of African life and culture: 'Battles are won before they begin./ Rehearse victory in faith and dreams.'

ന്ദ

Jennifer A. McGowan
How to be a Tarot Card, or a Teenager
Arachne Press, £9.99

McGowan uses the scaffold of the Tarot's Major Arcana to explore various life experiences, while 'teenager' may refer to the title poem: 'Don't be surprised/ if someone misreads you.'

The opening poem, 'The Real World' refers to 'the muted earth', and the question of what reality means seems to be an underlying theme. The poem 'Sign', wherein the narrator practises sign language, suggests a willingness to express what is unvoiced. 'The Lights Went Off' mentions '1485' (death of Richard III, who is arguably unjustly portrayed in many historical accounts), while 'Deaths of the Salem Witches' asks the question 'Did the condemned cry?'

There are also conflicting repeated images, on the one hand of smiling and laughter, on the other, of red and anger. All this intriguingly suggests that the poems want to offer an alternative viewpoint.

In 'Dr Wick' the reader learns the narrator lives with chronic disabilities: '*You'll be in a wheelchair before you're forty,/* the doctor warned./ I was sixteen. Could not walk without pain.' The narrator adds, 'I am sixty-four', bringing to mind the Beatles' song[1].

Pain presents itself both somatically and emotionally, and one poem I found particularly moving was 'The Boy who went back to Singapore': 'I was reborn to the taste of your skin/ that June when we collided,/ as if by accident, at university', but the relationship falters when 'my father died, anchored me/ to a lifetime of paperwork', then, 'last year your Facebook message/ made me cry. You send me all your love/ sent pictures of your daughter'. The regret feels tangible.

Some longer poems read like fables. In 'Horse-face and Ox-head', 'The moral is: Be just. Be true.' while in 'Why Snakes are Always Female' a princess befriends a snake which says, 'snakes moult their skin, leaving all past mistakes/ and sadnesses with their old one'.

McGowan's poems are also greatly enjoyable for their language, musicality, intertextuality and soundscape, such as 'Putting on 15th Century Clothing Blindfolded': 'First the shift. Linen drifts', 'a murrey kirtle, red purple, soft wood'.

The closing poem, 'Universe' has a bee 'pollinating a new planet'; XXI in the Tarot suggests the end of a cycle, to begin again with 'The Fool', but of course Tarot readings, like poems, are open to interpretation.

ཀྭ

Mukahang Limbu
Mother of Flip-Flops
OutSpoken Press, £8

This debut pamphlet relates the experiences of a young Nepalese-born man who moved to Britain with his family when he was ten, and these coming-of-age poems open with the title poem recalling the poet's childhood. This is a loving song to his mother with her 'chipped nail varnish on ginger fingers' and her 'smile/ the largest room in this house where/ we kill cockroaches' but it is also his 'Mother of// learning too early to be a mother'. Several poems focus on the hard life his mother subsequently endured, such as 'The Cleaners', written in her voice: 'HONEYMOON SUITE// WE ARE THE CLEANERS eating dust   we pick up/ dead skin in lumps along the inch of our fingers', and in 'The Cleaner's Wedding', when 'the Cleaner'

---

[1] Paul McCartney wrote 'When I'm Sixty-four', exploring what love might be like in old age, when he was a teenager (https://americansongwriter.com/what-paul-mccartney-regretted-about-the-beatles-when-im-sixty-four/)

mops the aisle 'With arms/ around her groom's grey plastic spine, they/ start to sway to a dance'.

At the heart of the book, the narrator imagines himself talking to his mother about 'how my father is unfortunately/ still alive,' and about 'the boy who sat on the carpet with me, his smile so close' ('Instead'). The pamphlet continues with poems exploring shame and queerness, such as 'where do all the Nepalese gay boys go', about boys on the cusp of adulthood, for example in, 'boys smell' 'the smell of *boy* moulting pubes *boy* plucking armpits/ in handfuls *boy* shaving off the queer boy days without a/ shower *boy* dripping grease brylcreem'. There is an unflinching honesty in this writing.

The poet also writes tenderly about his grandmother 'singing for the ghost   of her husband':

> still limping around his home
>> of pepper trees   monkeys   built   from
>
>> ~~fighting~~ fighting
> for the white man – the dead Gurkha

In addition to exotic images recalling his Nepalese boyhood, Limbu's forms are adventurous, with anaphora, strike-through, capitals and impactful line breaks. There is also a sense of resolution in the closing poem, 'Grownups', which ends, 'there is nothing a father can teach a son/ who has learned to walk all alone/ like a grown up.'

৩২৩

Shazea Quraishi
The Glimmer
Bloodaxe, £10.99

Quraishi is a Pakistani-born Canadian poet who lives in London. Her extended-narrative poems span the month she spent in an artist's colony in Mexico. Poems are in the voices of the many creatives she encountered, such as a miniaturist, a dancer who worked with Pina Bausch, a singer, and, predominately, the taxidermist. In place of titles the poems are sequenced by the days of the month.

'Day 1' introduces the taxidermist arranging her tools: 'scalpel tweezers   calipers/ pins   pipecleaners   wire   scissors/ needle   thread straw' as she meditates on her work.

Day 5

she takes the hummingbird from the freezer.
The boy down the road found it under a hibiscus bush,
they like red flowers.

Other poems include verbatim text from artists who are wrestling with self-doubt. '*It goes on and on the questioning*'. The end-notes identify this as being by the war photographer, Don McCullin. And, from Kwame Kwei-Armah:

> *Ultimately, you*
> *have to look at yourself and say*
> *Have I done the thing*
> *I set out to do?*

At her launch Quraishi said she likes to secrete aspects of her own life events into her poems, blending fact, truth and fiction. She explained she swam a lot during the composition of the book, so much of her thinking occurred underwater, even the title came from the sun glimmering on the pool floor, as if embodying hope. The poems also reference personal loss, 'she tries to remember her brother's voice/ the quiet of it'.

Quraishi often utilises formal constraints. The poems about animals brought in for taxidermy become anagrams of their title, such as 'White Mouse', reflecting the process of 'taking apart/ putting together'.

A particularly disturbing poem for me was 'Idol, doll' referencing a historic practice whereby

> Sometimes live birds
> were enclosed in the hollow body of dolls.
> Their frantic efforts to free themselves
> gave the doll the appearance of being alive

Although a little more contextual narrative would have been welcome, her launch provided this and added layers of richness to the poems I might otherwise have missed. Poems in *The Glimmer* have a mesmeric quality, offering wisdom and quiet reflection on life/death and creativity, and something beyond, like 'seeing sound'.

ෆෆ

Clare Shaw
Towards a General Theory of Love
Bloodaxe, £10.99

Shaw's fourth collection contains poignant, compelling poems. The title refers to a textbook of a similar name[2] and an epigraph references Harlow's monkey experiments[3] preparing the reader for an exploration of love, loss, and longing.

The collection opens with the poem, 'What the Frog Taught Me About Love', perhaps acknowledging our human-animal nature, and hinting that love might be first known by its absence. In 'Morecambe Bay as Grief', with its epigraph by Julian Barnes that 'Grief is the negative image of love', coming to terms with grief is brilliantly depicted as trying to drain the bay with its infamously treacherous quicksands and fast-rising tides. At the same time, the witty 'Love as a SatNav' reminds us 'love is not a reliable book... it insists you need it'.

Shaw considers many aspects of love. 'Monkey Writes a Poem About His Mother' shows how idealisation can follow trauma: 'You were the oak leaf and honey and clover' and ends with the heart-breaking line, referencing the Harlow experiments, 'You were not wire. You were not wire.' The narrator's mother features in early poems and these suggest a complex transgenerational relationship. Patterns however can be broken, and the speaker's decision to become a mother is followed by an imagined conversation with her newborn: 'And you ask would I die for you,/ a thousand times over.' Contrasting with this tender maternal love is the poem, 'In My Bedroom', with its devastating line, 'If you leave a baby long enough/ it learns not to cry.'

Shaw displays a mastery of form in her poems, together with music and language to enhance content. One example of this is found in 'An Empirical Examination of the Stage Theory of Grief', with its four-beat lines of short rhythmic sentences and cesurae in nearly all but the last stanza, where there is 'A small patch of dirt in the shape of my mother'. This seems to echo how grief can be worked through despite regular setbacks, until it can be laid to rest. In 'The Garden of Earthly Delights', there is a similar, if more joyous rhythmical lyricism: 'we lay in the grass and you smelt of sun/ and what happened between us was holy'.

The monkey trope appears in about one-third of the poems. Sometimes the narrator is a psychotherapist. In 'Monkey and I Discuss the

---

[2] *A General Theory of Love*, Thomas Lewis, Fari Amini and Richard Lannon (Random House, 2000)

[3] *Total social isolation in monkeys*, HF Harlow, RO Dodsworth and MK Harlow, Proc Natl Acad Sci US 1965 Jul; 54(1): 90–971965

83

Difficulty of Working Therapeutically with Non-Verbal Traumatic Memories' the abject isolation of early neglect is summed up thus: 'If I could put words to it, says Monkey,/ that would be half the problem solved.' In other poems the roles are reversed. In 'Monkey Teaches Me Map-reading Skills' the narrator confides she has met a woman, 'we were lost' and 'I am in Love'. In 'Monkey invites Me to Imagine' the narrator is walking in snow 'and my paws are bare [...]' 'Sometimes I don't know which of us/ is monkey'.

Love's multifarious possibilities are also reflected in the titles, 'Love as DIY', 'Love as a Global Pandemic' and 'Love as a Poem' with its clever line, 'We were a villanelle, we kept going/ in circles'.

In 'Night Swimming, Derwentwater', the poet writes: 'The cold is a hurt// we return to, over and over', perhaps suggesting loss is integral to love. The power of love to transform is captured in a poem I intend to read regularly: 'Everything Is a Gift', reminding the reader there is something beneficial to learn from all experiences, and our arrival in the world prepares us for this: 'the scream is the language of life'.

∾

Nóra Blascsók
<body>of work</body>
Broken Sleep Books, £4

Nóra Blascsók's debut pamphlet follows her highly original 'Legitimate Snack 23' from Broken Sleep in 2021 and offers a sharply observed, wry take on corporate life, both working from home during the pandemic and subsequently returning to the office.

The title 'Fizz and excitement' is taken from the poem's epigraph by Jeremy Hunt, which is a quotation from a speech by the then-Health Secretary referring to 'the fizz and excitement that you get in a really good work place'. The poet's use of forward slashes to break up the prose poem creates a feeling of exhaustion that works well with the irony of the words: 'recall that feeling / of entering / honey / I'm home'.

One of Blascsók's particular skills is her use of sparklingly inventive form. 'Wearing my skin to work' is laid out like a timetable, with the weekdays boxed in, containing images of clothing for each day which become increasingly unkempt as the week unfolds. The luckless narrator starts out 'crisp like /steamed / over hot/ bath' but by Friday has slumped to 'tits on/ keyboard' [...] 'unbutton for'.

Erasure poems are included in the poet's repertoire giving the sense of what is not seen, thus aptly depicting office life, as in this last line of the opening poem of the book, '*Minding the gap*'. This poem uses text taken from Dettol's 'back to work' advertisements that went viral on social media in 2020: '███ little ███ we do ████████ little ███ we love. Keep ██████ '.

These are funny yet moving poems that cleverly convey the sense of isolation and being lost that can accompany the corporate world. In 'Plants' the poet communicates with her wilting houseplant by the north-facing window. The 'purple-blue' plant echoes the poet's bruised feelings as she puts on her brave face and writes, 'I feel for them/ trapped with me. I lean close and whisper: we're going to be fine.'

∞

Katie O'Pray
Apricot
OutSpoken Press, £11.99

O'Pray is described in press releases as using poetry to explore different identities: being 'queer, a trauma survivor, an addict, having mental issues, suffering from Diabetes 1'. The courage it must have taken to write these poems suggests O'Pray is feisty and determined to fight. Nevertheless, the poems in the third section, which appear to quote verbatim commentary from health authority consultants, are shocking to read:

> —but the likelihood that you will — drop — down
> dead
>   is statistically high — we are simply concerned
> you won't make it through the weekend—

The book comprises four sections, with the first concerning the names the narrator goes by and considering aspects of queerness, diabetes and food (references to food appear in about two-thirds of the poems). The second section explores the support the speaker received, with friends' names as titles, in parenthesis, which cleverly depicts the sense of isolation actually experienced. The third section, '*IS YOUR ILLNESS OLD ENOUGH TO HOLD A SENTENCE?*' informs the reader of the chronic nature of their problems, while the final section, '*WHERE DO YOU THINK YOU WILL SURVIVE*' looks with hope at what the future might hold, such as 'on the good days'.

I felt a mounting sense of anxiety as I read the collection, possibly engendered in part by the form and language of the poems. The poet employs language that is often fractured, with forward slashes and presented in an urgent address, sometimes in capitals. The final section feels calmer,

85

as if some kind of resolution has been reached. In 'under branches', they write: 'I want to eat the sky today/ broad door of it open,'. The final poem, 'back home' finds the speaker 'laying down in snow suddenly   I was twenty two' and the poem ends on the fighting note: 'I came out of the sickness/ like a sore loser/ saying: *okay, I'm ready, I'll bite*'.

Finally the title. I couldn't find a specific reference to apricots in any poem, and half-wondered if it referenced Czeslaw Milosz's 'Gathering Apricots', about loss and survivor-guilt, but a Google search revealed the apricot is a symbol of hope and optimism, which offers a positive conclusion to this powerful book.

Mary Mulholland

Contributors

Barbara Barnes' poems have appeared in *Poetry London, Butcher's Dog, Ambit, Interpreter's House, Under the Radar, Brixton Review of Books, Perverse*, and *The Alchemy Spoon*; also in *For the Silent, Cry of the Poor, Crooked Jukebox* and *Invitation to Love*. Her collection, *Hound Mouth*, was published by Live Canon in 2022.

Heidi Beck emigrated to the UK from the USA in 1998 and now lives in Bristol. She has worked as a tour guide, data analyst and assistant zookeeper. Recent poems have appeared in *Poetry Ireland Review, Rialto, Magma, Finished Creatures, The Alchemy Spoon* and online at *The Friday Poem*. **www.heidibeck.com**

Jennifer Ben-Ali is an alternative therapist based in Preston Lancashire. She loves meditation and other spiritual practices. Her photographs can be found on *Instagram* @jenbenali.

Liz Berry was born in the Black Country and lives in Birmingham. Her books have been Poetry Book Society Recommendations. She has received a Somerset Maugham Award, the Geoffrey Faber Memorial Award and Forward Prize for Best First Collection, together with Forward Prize for Best Single Poem. *Home Child* will be published in 2023.

Julian Bishop's first collection of eco poems called *We Saw It All Happen* is out in early 2023 from Fly On The Wall Press. A former environment reporter for the BBC, he is a former runner-up in the Ginkgo Prize for Eco Poetry.

Corinna Board teaches English as an additional language in Oxford. She grew up on a farm and is particularly inspired by nature. Her poems have appeared in various journals including *Green Ink, Anthropocene* and *Spelt*. Her debut pamphlet is due in 2023. Find her on Instagram @parole_de_reveuse or Twitter @CorinnaBoard.

Claire Booker is a medical herbalist who lives near Brighton. Her poems have appeared most recently in *Poetry Birmingham, Dark Horse, Magma, Mslexia, Under the Radar* and on Worthing Pier. Her first full collection, *A Pocketful of Chalk*, is out with Arachne Press**.** www.bookerplays.co.uk

Jane Burn is an award-winning, working class, pansexual, autistic person, parent, poet, artist, essayist, and off-grid enthusiast. Her poems are widely published and anthologised. Jane has an MA in Writing Poetry from Newcastle University/The Poetry School. Her latest collection, *Be Feared*, is available from Nine Arches.

Katie Byford is a former Barbican Young Poet and was the winner of the Oxford Brookes International Poetry Competition in 2020. Her first pamphlet, *He Said I Was a Peach*, was published in 2021 with ignitionpress. Her work has been published in *Magma, bath magg* and *Modern Poetry in Translation*.

Diana Cant is a child psychotherapist with an MA in Poetry. She has been published in various anthologies and magazines. Her pamphlet, *Student Bodies 1968*, was published by Clayhanger Press, and her second pamphlet, *At Risk – the lives some children live*, was published by Dempsey & Windle in 2021.

Pratibha Castle's award-winning debut pamphlet *A Triptych of Birds and A Few Loose Feathers* was published 2022. Published in *Agenda, HU, Blue Nib, IS&T, London Grip, OHC, Friday Poem, High Window*, highly commended, longlisted in competitions including The Bridport Prize, she was given special mention in The Welsh Poetry Competition.

Rachael Clyne, from Glastonbury, came late to publishing poetry. Her collection, *Singing at the Bone Tree*, concerns environmental issues. Rachael's pamphlet, *Girl Golem*, explores a migrant Jewish heritage. Her collection, *You'll Never Be Anyone Else*, to be published by Seren in 2023, explores identity in childhood, sexual orientation and ageing.

Kerry Darbishire lives in Cumbria. She has two pamphlets one with Dempsey & Windle, one with Grey Hen Press. Two full poetry collections with IDP and a third collection recently published by Hedgehog Press. Her poems have appeared widely in anthologies and magazines and have been placed in competitions.

Hélène Demetriades' debut collection *The Plumb Line* was published by Hedgehog Press in June 2022. She is also the winner of the Silver Wyvern, Poetry On The Lake, 2022. She works as a transpersonal psychotherapist, and began writing poetry in midlife. Her work has been published in journals and anthologies.

Luciana Francis is originally from São Paulo, Brazil. She moved to the UK in 1998. Her debut poetry pamphlet, *Travel Writing*, is out now, published by Against the Grain Poetry Press. Her poetry has been recently shortlisted for the Bridport Prize. She is a member of the collective Voicing Our Silences, founded by Alice Hiller.

SK Grout (she/they) is an editor and writer who grew up in Aotearoa New Zealand, lived in Germany and now splits her time between London and Auckland Tāmaki Makaurau. Her debut chapbook is *What love would smell like* (V. Press, 2021). https://skgroutpoetry.wixsite.com/poetry.

Rachel Goodman was formerly an actor and BBC presenter. She moved back to Norfolk 25 years ago to raise a family and to write. She has been shortlisted twice for the Bridport prize and won or been placed in many other competitions. She has been published in many journals.

Emma Gray is a neurodivergent writer and artist from Brighton, UK. Her work has been shortlisted for the Creative Future Writers' Award in 2021, longlisted for the Mslexia Poetry Competition 2022 and published by *Bivouac*, *Wildfire Words* and CityLit's *Between the Lines 2022*.

Carole Greenfield grew up in Colombia and lives in New England. Her work has appeared in *Sparks of Calliope, Sky Island Journal, The Plenitudes* and *Dodging the Rain*, among others.

Steve Harrison from Yorkshire now lives in Shropshire. His work has been published widely in *The Emergency Poet* collections, *Pop Shot*, *Wetherspoons News*, *Strix* and on YouTube as steveharrison poet. He performs across the Midlands and won the Ledbury Poetry Festival Slam in 2014.

Rennie Halstead writes poetry, short fiction and poetry reviews. He lives in Kent.

Robin Helweg-Larsen is Anglo-Danish by birth and Bahamian by upbringing, and has been published in the *Alabama Literary Review, Allegro, Ambit, Amsterdam Quarterly*, etc. He is Series Editor for Sampson Low's *Potcake Chapbooks - Form in Formless Times,* and blogs at formalverse dot com from his hometown of Governor's Harbour.

Lucy Ingrams has won the Manchester Poetry Prize, the Magma poetry prize and the Ware Poets prize. Her pamphlet, *Light-fall*, is published by Flarestack Poets.

John Lancaster has had five poetry collections published including *The Barman* (Smith/Doorstop) and *Potters: A Division Of Labour* (Longmarsh Press) which won the inaugural Arnold Bennett Book Prize 2017. A past runner-up in the National Poetry Competition, originally from Stoke-on-Trent, he lives in Devon.

Sharon Larkin's books include *Interned at the Food Factory* (Indigo Dreams, 2019) and *Dualities* (Hedgehog, 2020). Individual poems have been published by *Magma, Cinnamon, Eyewear, Prole, Yaffle, Dreich, Ink Sweat & Tears, Atrium* and more. Sharon runs Eithon Bridge Publications and Good Dadhood. She is Gloucestershire's Stanza Representative. https://sharonlarkinjones.com

Hannah Linden's most recent awards are 1st prize in the Cafe Writers Open Poetry Competition 2021 and Highly Commended in the Poetry Wales Award 2021. *The Beautiful Open Sky* with V. Press is her debut pamphlet and she is working towards her first full collection. Twitter: @hannahl1n

Eric Machan Howd (Ithaca, NY) is a poet, musician, and educator. His fifth collection of poems, *Universal Monsters*, was recently published by The Orchard Street Press. He is currently working on an erasure project using the works of author H.P. Lovecraft.

John Martin's 2004 collection, *The Origin of Loneliness*, was followed by poems in *The London Magazine, Magma, The Lancet, Dreich, Trasna, Drawn to the Light* and *Ink Drinkers* magazines. A former soldier, he studied philosophy before medicine and currently works as a doctor and scientist in Europe and the US.

Margot Myers, retired bookseller, lives in Oxford. She has a PhD on fairy tales and writes in genres both light and dark. She has been placed or commended in several competitions, and widely published in magazines and anthologies. *I Meant to Say* (2020) is her debut pamphlet. https://www.poetshousepamphlets.co.uk

Kate Noakes is a PhD student at the University of Reading researching contemporary British and American poetry. Her eighth collection, *Goldhawk Road*, will be published by Two Rivers Press in February 2023. She lives in London and when not writing is a print maker.

Emmaline O'Dowd lives in Derby and is pleased not to be teaching music anymore. Her work has appeared in a range of magazines, most recently *Acumen, Orbis* and *Pennine Platform* (forthcoming).

Niall M. Oliver lives in Ireland with his wife and sons. He is the author of *My Boss* by Hedgehog Poetry. His poems have featured in *Acumen, Atrium, The Honest Ulsterman, Fly On The Wall Press, Ink Sweat & Tears* and others.

Martin Rieser is published in *Poetry Review, Magma 74, The Alchemy Spoon, morphrog*, was highly Commended for Norman Nicholson Prize and Artlyst Ekphrastic anthology, shortlisted for Frosted Fire Firsts and longlisted for Charles Causley 2019 and Erbacce Prize 2021. First prize in the Hastings Literary Festival 2021.

Gillie Robic was born in India and lives in London. She is widely published in magazines and anthologies, with two collections from Live Canon, *Swimming Through Marble* and *Lightfalls,* and a new pamphlet, *Open Skies* in aid of Ukraine.

Finola Scott's poems scatter on the wind, landing in places such as *The High Window, New Writing* Scotland, *Ink Sweat & Tears* and *Lighthouse.* Red Squirrel Press publish *Much left unsaid.* Dreich publish *Count the ways,* Tapsalteerie publish *Modern Makars: Yin.* Finola enjoys dancing in her kitchen. Visit at Finola Scott Poems FB

Paul Stephenson has three poetry pamphlets: *Those People* (Smith/Doorstop, 2015), which won the Poetry Business pamphlet competition; *The Days that Followed Paris* (HappenStance, 2016), written after the November 2015 terrorist attacks; and *Selfie with Waterlilies* (Paper Swans Press, 2017). He helps curate Poetry in Aldeburgh. Website: paulstep.com / Instagram: paulstep456

Pam Thompson is a writer and educator based in Leicester. Her publications include *The Japan Quiz* (Redbeck Press, 2009) and *Show Date and Time* (Smith | Doorstop, 2006) and *Strange Fashion* (Pindrop Press, 2017). She is a 2019 Hawthornden Fellow.

Carl Tomlinson lives on a smallholding in Oxfordshire. His first pamphlet, *Changing Places* was published by Fair Acre Press in 2021. His work has been published in magazines and online. His poem 'Market Forces' forms part of the audio guide to Oxford's Covered Market.

Sue Wallace-Shaddad has an MA from Newcastle University. Dempsey & Windle published her pamphlet, *A City Waking Up,* October 2020. Recently shortlisted for the Plough Prize, her poems feature in many online and print publications. Sue is Secretary of Suffolk Poetry Society. https://suewallaceshaddad.wordpress.com

Tim Waller, published in the U.K. and in the U.S., taught theatre, speech, and English in Illinois. Favourite writers include Emily Dickinson and Richard Blanco. Currently, he is working on his first poetry collection.

Rob Walton is from Scunthorpe, and lives in Whitley Bay. His poems and flash fictions have been published in the UK, USA, Canada, Ireland and New Zealand. He sometimes tweets: @robwaltonwriter.

Spencer Wood (he /him) is a poet and teacher based in Leeds. His work has been published in *Untitled Voices, Modern Queer Poets* and upcoming in *14 Poems*. Spencer recently read at the Leeds Poetry Festival and he runs the monthly LGBTQ+ Drama Club for Leeds Community Consortium.

Kate Young's poetry has appeared in various webzines/magazines nationally and in Canada. It has also featured in the anthologies *Places of Poetry* and *Write Out Loud*. Her pamphlet, *A Spark in the Darkness,* is published by Hedgehog Press. Find her on Twitter @Kateyoung12poet.

Submission Guidelines

We welcome submissions of up to three brilliant, unpublished, original poems on the issue's theme through the website during the submission window. You will find full details of how to submit on our website: www.alchemyspoon.org.

We are only able to accept submissions from those over 18.

If you have poems published in the current issue of *The Alchemy Spoon*, then we ask that you wait out one issue before submitting more work.

Simultaneous submissions are permitted but please tell us straightaway if a poem is accepted for publication elsewhere.

We aim for a speedy turn-round and will respond to every submission, but we don't offer individual feedback.

Authors retain all rights. However, if a poem is then published elsewhere, please acknowledge that it first appeared in *The Alchemy Spoon*.

Our submission window for Issue 9 will be open 1 – 28 February, 2023, the theme for the issue will be 'Graffiti' and we will welcome poems on this theme up to 40 lines. See our website for the full details.

Submission Guidelines for Essays
If you have an essay on some cutting-edge poetry-related topic, please send it to us during the submission window for consideration +/- 1500 words.

Submission Guidelines for Artwork
We are always looking for original artwork to feature on future magazine covers. Portrait-orientated images work best (or images suitable for cropping). Good quality lower resolution images can be sent at the submission stage, but higher res files will be needed (2480 pixels x 3508 pixels) at print stage.

Submission Guidelines for Reviews
If you would like to recommend a poetry collection or submit a review of a collection, then please email us or use the contact form on the website.

Poetry Workshops
The Alchemy Spoon editors offer a one-to-one poetry feedback and workshopping service without prejudice via Zoom or Facetime. All profits from this contribute to the cost of running Clayhanger Press. Please email vanessa.tas@btinternet.com to arrange this.

Cover Design by Clayhanger Press

Typesetting and Design Roger Bloor
Senior Copy Editor Sara Levy
Proof-reader Adam Lampert

www.clayhangerpress.co.uk

Clayhanger Press

Printed in Great Britain
by Amazon

15038328R00058